Branding the Teleself

Branding the Teleself

Media Effects Discourse and the Changing Self

ERNEST A. HAKANEN

LEXINGTON BOOKS

A division of
ROWMAN & LITTLEFIELD PUBLISHERS, INC.
Lanham • Boulder • New York • Toronto • Plymouth, UK

LEXINGTON BOOKS

A division of Rowman & Littlefield Publishers, Inc.
A wholly owned subsidiary of The Rowman & Littlefield Publishing Group, Inc.
4501 Forbes Boulevard, Suite 200
Lanham, MD 20706

Estover Road
Plymouth PL6 7PY
United Kingdom

British Library Cataloguing in Publication Information Available

Library of Congress Cataloging-in-Publication Data

Hakanen, Ernest A.
  Branding the teleself : media effects discourse and the changing self / Ernest A.
Hakanen.
     p. cm.
  Includes bibliographical references.
  ISBN-13: 978-0-7391-1733-0 (cloth : alk. paper)
  ISBN-10: 0-7391-1733-5 (cloth : alk. paper)
  1. Mass media—Social aspects. 2. Self. I. Title.
  HM1206.H33 2007
  302.2301—dc22   2007017518

Printed in the United States of America

™
⊖ The paper used in this publication meets the minimum requirements of American
National Standard for Information Sciences—Permanence of Paper for Printed Library
Materials, ANSI/NISO Z39.48–1992.

Contents

Figures   vii

Acknowledgements   ix

Introduction: Branding the Teleself   1

1   Branded: An Essay on the Teleself   7

2   Tools for Analysis: Social Psychology   15
     as History, the Social Grid, and Kuhn's Influence
     on Media Effects History

3   The Passive Self   35

4   The Active Self   49

5   The Commodified Self   61

6   A Turn to the Teleself   71

7   Ferment of the Teleself: Releasing the Free Agent   93

Appendix: Poststructuralism and Critical Theory   101

References   117

Index   123

Figures

Figure 2.1. Media Effects Model   25

Figure 2.2. Opposing Paradigms   32

Figure 3.1. Dominant Paradigms and the Self   35

Figure 6.1. Consequences of Agenda Setting   79

Figure 6.2. The Dependency Model   87

Figure A.1. Semiotics of Peirce   103

Figure A.2. Semiosis   103

Acknowledgements

I wish to thank Drexel University for giving me support and a leave of absence to start this book at the Critical Theory Institute at the University of California, Irvine. At Drexel, I wish to thank my undergraduate honors students for putting up with my formative ideas in our music and communication course. I especially want to thank Lyz Zaffrano and Rob Amerman for their discussions of the ideas. Tony Trumbo gets a special thanks for not only discussing the ideas but suggesting the title of the book. Rich Bowen and Ron Bishop also gave me very useful background suggestions though their close readings.

Introduction

Branding the Teleself

Branding is a term used and, seemingly, understood universally. Branding, in short, is the identity of a product that adds value to the product. Discussions of branding usually lead to the conclusion that brands are often more important these days than the product they represent. It may also be argued that brands are bought and sold regardless of their product. The importance of branding to the producer is obvious. What has become more obvious is the consumers' desire to want brands that, in turn, they use to represent themselves.

Although Naomi Klein (2002) and others have popularized the notion in books and films, the notion of a "branded" self goes back to the 1930s with Max Horkheimer and Theodor Adorno (1987), who used the term to define the mass culturally-constructed self.

> Anyone who goes cold and hungry, even if his prospects were once good, is branded. He is an outsider; and apart from certain capital crimes, the most mortal of sins is to become an outsider.

In the spirit of the critical theory and the era in which it thrived, being branded was a fear mechanism that structured our lives. The quote is about conforming to social structures.

I believe that Americans have gone a step further and branded themselves in order to deliver themselves to the market. I use the term to define the fact that today we brand ourselves as "unique." We believe that we are unique selves, that we have free choice to be unique and to choose in general. However, I believe that we brand ourselves in relation to a market that defines this unique character. Simply put, "unique" is defined for us, it is a market category as are

1

all others. To go further than those of critical theory, I believe that we knowingly commodify ourselves. Product, advertising, Madison Avenue, or whatever metaphor you wish to use, does not commodify us. We deliver ourselves very aggressively to the market. Commodification is no longer in the power of the product differentiation. Commodification is a belief system that we can differentiate ourselves for the market. That notion comes from how we discuss our relationship with media. I intend to show this in a unique way.

I believe that we can trace the changes in the notion of the self through a close examination of the public discourse in the history of mass media effects. By the history of media effects, I mean the way in which the story of the scholarly study of the interaction between mass media and society has been told. By the construction of the self, I mean how individuals represent as social beings. Through an examination of how and why the media effects story has been told, changes in the construction of the self in the media age will be examined. In other words, I will use the way we have thought about ourselves vis-a-vis the way we believe the media affect us to show the development of a new kind of notion of the self that I call the teleself.

But how does a reading of the history of mass media effects give us insight into the nature of the contemporary self? The story of media effects has generally been told from the social psychological point of view, in which approaches that use experimental, empirical, scientific methods are favored. Even alternative histories that argue against the dominant point of view use the social psychological point of view as a means of comparison and departure. Kenneth Gergen argues (1973) that social psychology is really more of a history than a science. He believes that any experimentation involving human subjects is a communication system. At one level, the subject is always acting within the boundaries created by the researcher, at least in the researcher's eyes. Therefore, the subject is creating a message to be decoded by the researcher. The researcher decodes the message within a framework that is driven usually by the important topics of the day and then fed back to the public, thereby reinforcing boundaries in the culture. This is especially powerful in a mass mediated society in which cause and effect results are received by a much larger public than previously. Therefore, the telling of the tale, the discourse, is a very accurate way of describing the culturally important topics and how individuals act within the framework set. Hence, social psychologists are "engaged in a systematic account of contemporary affairs—history-making" (p. 316). Beyond the interaction of social scientists and subjects is a history of a discipline that (re)makes itself based on its history. Michel Foucault argues that these histories themselves structure the evolution of the self in a process called the "history of now."

What better place, then, than in social psychology, especially the area that looks at media effects, to look for the contemporary self, changes in the notion of self, or possibly the erasure of the self? Almost all of the theoretical literature about the self attributes shifts, changes, mutations, deletions, etc., directly to the content of the media or to the media's role in the commercialization or commodification of the self. By examining the history of media effects, we may be able to recognize changes in the construction of the self.

What is more, the tidiness of the history of media effects makes it a good archeological site. The narrative of media effects is greatly influenced by Thomas Kuhn (1971). Kuhn's idea that science develops in spurts that are influenced by challenges to belief systems, called paradigms, has greatly influenced historians of science. This is especially true of the history of mass media effects, because as other fields reviewed their histories with a Kuhnian history, the new field of mass media effects began telling its history post-Kuhn. This process has led to a very tidy, yet exaggerated history. For example, the structure and shifts within the history are widely agreed upon, not necessarily as fact, but as the point of departure for most discussions of the topic. And it is delightfully exaggerated to the verge of parody, as at least three paradigm shifts have been declared in only the last sixty years.

The time period of media effects studies coincides with the debate of the nature of the self in modern and postmodern societies. Most postmodern thinkers address the topic directly at a theoretical level. Foucault provoked discussion about the self by arguing that the notion of the self did not exist until the modern age when individuality and self-awareness were born. Postmodernism focuses to a "great extent on the emerging new individual identity or subject position, one that abandons what may, in retrospect, be the narrow scope of the modern individual with its claim to rationality and autonomy" (Poster, 1996, 1). Jean Baudrillard, among countless others, identifies media content as the determinant force in the creation of a new commodified self. Foucault, Baudrillard, and Mark Poster, along with neo-McLuhanists such as Neil Postman, see the self as a product of a new language or discourse that emphasizes the subjective rather than objective position of the past. The new discourse is driven by the dominant medium of the period or era.

Now, why is such an endeavor important? Trying to find evidence for a contemporary self opens up even more ground for study and debate. The debates are endless. So, as I've already said, I will not take that course. I believe, however, that the mass media, especially television, have played a large role in the construction of the self. Now, obviously my readers are saying that this topic of the media's relationship to the construction of the self is huge and a bit too deterministic, and they are right. My quest is more specific.

I take a different tack on relationship of the construction of self to media. Above all, this book looks at the discourse of media effects and its very impact on the construction of the self. In the most simple terms, my argument is that how media effects are discussed over time critically impacts the way we think about ourselves as human beings and how the discourse is shaped by the constructs of the self. Simply put, there is no cause here. There is however a very important relationship that I wish to point out and that is the relationship between the discourse of how people are affected by the media and how they think about what constitutes a self.

I believe that this bond has strengthened to new level. Each medium not only envelops the ones that preceded it, but also become more ubiquitous than the last. However, I argue that it is neither the medium nor the message of the medium that affects us. It is the discourse about the our relationship with the media that change the language about ourselves and our position that constructs the self. And as the discourse becomes more prominent in the general social discourse, the construction of the self cannot help but change. I argue that the social grid upon which we place ourselves and develop our identities is made up of the discourse about the self and its relationship to and with media.

I would like to show how the historical construction of the discourse of media effects has radically eased us into very different selves. Television effects studies, in particular, have taken us from describing ourselves as passive viewers to active viewers to hyperactive viewers in six decades of the television age. I will describe these developments in a history of the discourse of media effects. I come to the conclusion that we have developed a hyper language, one that surpasses previous forms of logic and is much more emotionally based. My thesis is the reverse of a so-called "couch potato phenomenon," which sees television as creating a passive viewer. I believe that television and its "known" effects have given us the illusion of free choice with it and our world. This language and its illusions and the resultant new selves have not gone unnoticed by social theorists, mainly those described as postmodernists.

This uncovering of this illusion is what makes the present study important. First, media effects discourse can be revealed as a force in the construction of the self. Second, this seemingly liberating information can have contradictory effect on not just the construction of the self, but the notion of free will. Third, I will try not to make any value judgments regarding this changed notion of the self, but we must question where it leads.

The residual effects of this study are two. First, although I will try to present a reading of the history of media effects in search of the self and promise not to look for the "true" history (the "true" history is the one that has been public in our case), at times the structure, especially events labeled paradigm shifts or revolutions must be brought into question and discussed vis-a-vis Kuhn's expectations. Second, the approach of "social science as history" has a purpose to expand the theory, value, and, especially, relevance of experimental social sciences through self reflexivity. Therefore, it is hoped that the present study provides greater knowledge of our disciplines purpose.

Design of the Book

I will argue my thesis by showing how the the idea of "viewer" has been constructed at various levels. I will start with a discussion of the current age's use of language, in the form of the linguistic turn and poststructuralism, to show how modern philosophy has changed the notion of the self. I will focus more clearly on the poststructural literature that addresses the notion of viewer or the construction of the self in the age of information (e.g., Baudrillard, Poster, Foucault).

The media effects paradigm and the threat from competing paradigms will then be discussed at length to show how this type of discourse or reconstruction of the historical discourse of the viewer has also painted regardless of the argument for a passive or active viewer as a hyperactive viewer, or the one we will come to know as "branded." I will show how the poststructural or postmodern viewer is a product of the shifts in interpretation of Marshall McLuhan's ideas, cybernetics (Norbert Wiener), and the information model (Claude Shannon and Warren Weaver), right through to the debates and research on the nature of the viewer.

I will define, eventually, the new teleself as a believer in the idea that he is now the sender of all messages, and no longer the receiver of messages whose only response is reduced to feedback. The illusion of sending all messages is false. The viewer is hopelessly vulnerable. Then, I want to go beyond theorizing about the teleself. I argue that these approaches to defining audiences, and especially media effects, are not isolated from the public and in large part help the viewer *cum* televiewer come to know himself. I believe that the messages sent to us on television effects have strengthened a free-agency argument. In other words, I argue a Foulcaultian view of these histories and descriptions as "histories of the now," not academic histories, but history that actually touches the real lives of real people. Simply put, how we describe ourselves is what we become or at least limits our descriptions of ourselves.

This particular history of media effects has been a particularly powerful social phenomenon. First, it is a very public history "as seen in the media" as it reports on its effects or, more than likely, lack thereof. Second, it is powerful because it has been institutionalized by the government and science. The government has often started and finished debates over the effects of the media. From the surgeon general's report on media violence of the 1970s to the Joe Camel controversies of the 1990s, the media is either the cause or the carrier of effect, both negative and positive. The media effects school is the social scientific, quantitative, and empirical arm of media studies. The school itself is an attempt to sell social understanding as science, as is true of all social sciences, as it attempts to gain recognition in our scientized society. Science is so historically powerful and cultural bound that it "sells" as the only valuable way of knowing.

The first chapter is in the form of an essay in which I develop the idea of the branded viewer, one that is defined as a teleself. The teleself reaches further and wider than ever before searching for itself. I want to first create a profile of what I want to argue toward. I stole this approach from Foucault, who often began pieces with a metaphorical essay on a practice, art, or art work. I believe this makes for a more readerly relationship to the text.

Then, in the second chapter, I will argue the notion of social psychology as history, which drive the inquiry. This is followed by a discussion of Foucault's and others idea of the grid and the evolving notion of audience. I will give a thumbnail sketch of the history of mass media effects research and shifts in paradigms.

Chapters three through seven cover the history of mass media effects with the purpose of giving empirical evidence for the changing notion of the self. Baudrillard links postmodern identity to product within a useful critical framework. His work provides me with a reading of media effects history from the stand point of not how it has been written but why it has been written. He also provides a template of a shifting self that not only fits the argument but I hope reinforces it. In the end, I wish to show that the teleself is not just an accidental construct of the postmodern age, but has been empirically evident in the so-called effects studies and related market research of the past few decades.

The appendix is a primer on how I marry two theoretical views, poststructural and critical theory, for their complementary powers of observation and explanation. At a very basic level, I believe that the poststructuralists are right in their observations about the postmodern self. However, I believe that they lack power of explanation for their observations. Therefore, they are easily refuted because they lack reason. A strong cultural theory that addresses popular culture provides these observations with explanatory power. By using a model of the commodified self that comes out of the Frankfurt School, we may attempt to understand the development and, therefore, the direction of the postmodern self.

Chapter One

My Branded: An Essay on the Teleself

Branded
(music by Dominic Frontiere, lyrics by Alan Alch)

All but one man died
There at Bitter Creek
And they say he ran away.

Branded,
Scorned as the one who ran.
What do you do when you're branded
And you know you're a man?

He was innocent.
Not a charge was true.
But the world will never know.

Branded,
Marked with a coward's shame.
What do you do when you're branded?
Well, you fight for your name.

Wherever you go for the rest of your life
You must prove
You're a man.

One of the first television shows I remember watching as a kid was *Branded*. The show, starring Chuck Connors, ran from January of 1965 to October 1966. The plot was the same every week: Colonel Jason McCord, falsely accused of abandoning his comrades during battle and stripped of his rank, roams the American West helping people but leaves town before the town's folk discover his shame.

I remember liking the show very much. I probably liked it because it was so predictable (which is also probably why the show had such a short run) and because it was about the West. Westerns were in and I was a great fan, joining my immigrant Finnish grandmother and great-uncle every Friday to watch *Wagontrain* and *Rawhide*.

I don't remember anything about the program's characters or more specific plots, only the general narrative. I only remember that someone who was shamed was attempting to fight for his character but, because of his unrevealed reputation, bound himself to be viewed as a coward. Nevertheless, the hero returned each and every week with the belief that he might have some effect on his fate, only to be roped back into social reality. The social reality was that there were no witnesses other than the hero himself.

As I look back, I can't imagine why a television program in which the hero could never win was put on the air. It was doomed from the the first episode. One would think that the writers would have opted for a *Lord Jim* or *Fugitive* narrative, in which witnesses or evidence are available to the hero somewhere, giving the viewer hope each week for the hero's redemption.

What I remember most about the show was its theme song. I don't think I'll get an argument from anyone who remembers the television series when I say that the show's theme song was unique. It opened with a cliched slow, dirge-like drum roll. The lyrics were sung by a chorus of monotoned baritones. The combination of drums and chorus sounded like surf music played at 16 1/2 RPM (For the CD generation, that's half-speed).

The opening scene for the first few seconds of the theme song was a close-up of the drum being beaten. Then, the camera cut to our hero being stripped of his cavalry stripes by his commanding officer in front of rows of observing comrades. Our shamed hero was then shown from behind walking out of the fort alone.

The shame of it all, the public shame. He was the only man—"All but one man died." Now he was alone heading toward the vast American West, the endless expanse of our country's manifest destiny. The image was strong. It supported the notion of an individualistic American taking all that is his—alone.

I can't forget those lyrics. They have been stuck in my head for more than thirty years. They are simple, yet so dramatic. The first verse was sung at a whisper. It sets the stage for the pain (of the remainder of the song and our hero), when the chorus strongly proclaims, "Branded!" representing the striking of a branding iron to the skin. The television viewer feels the pain of the outcast forced to be a lonely cowboy.

Mythic idealism is at the core of the American self (Bellah et al., 1985). This American hero must leave society in order to realize moral good. The cowboy-hero is a particularly good expression of the mythic hero. The great cowboys are constantly saving a society that the cowboy hemself can't fit into. The cowboy is too unique for his own good, too good for himself and everyone else. He defends a society that he cannot join. "The hero's lonely quest for moral excellence ends in absolute nihilism" (p. 146). He continues:

> in myth and . . . popular culture . . . we find the fear that society may overwhelm the individual and destroy any chance of autonomy unless he stands against it, but also recognition that it is only in relation to society that the individual can fulfill himself and that if the break with society is too radical, life has no meaning at all (p. 144).

The line "What do you do when you're branded and you know you're a man?" tells us that just being a man does not a member of society make. At the same time, maybe it means that a hero, a perfect man, can never belong. Beyond that, can our hero really believe he is a human being if he has no social being?

Nihilism completes the myth. Should our hero have died a real, morbid death rather than suffer his social death? If he had died, he would have been a hero, albeit a dead one among many dead ones. (Actually, I find it strange that we mythologize battles in which everyone died more than we do battles that we have won.) In the case of our hero, his life is not his reward. Only his dying could have been his reward. Therefore, the hero's rewards always go to society, rather than to the hero. The song and the cowboy myth teaches us, then, that the only real death in which humanness is taken away is social death. Social death is worse than physical death.

There is another point to be made, one that has to do with our nature as human beings and the power we have in the creation of our lives. Let's go back to our hero left to fight for his name. The most serious of social deaths is for no one to know you exist. This removes your name from the social grid, the matrix of names. Your name is important because it is what distinguishes you on the landscape of names. Our names or reputations create and are created by a very strong set of social assumptions and stereotypes. Bodies are similar, but names distinguish us from one another. We even speak of making a name for ourselves. But as the song says, "But the world would never know."

McCord's task is doubly difficult, if not outright impossible. First, there are no witnesses to his heroism. Winning back his name is impossible. Second, winning back a "new" name is just as impossible as it is illogical. As he attempts to fight for his name, he can only be seen as trying too hard—as "protesting too much." When anyone attempts to redefine themselves outside their socially perceived character, they come across in the eyes of others as incredulous or phony.

So, our hero without a name is not as human as other people. He has been reduced to a body. Bodies without souls or consciousness are cowards. By the same token, one who tries to remake himself is also a coward. Because his social name has been reduced to flesh, we treat him as a body, distinguished only by its markings. He is really branded—marked. Deeds can't free him. No matter what his actions, he will never win. So, being branded not only suggests that he is socially rejected; he is reduced to just his own flesh. Never having to gain approval is not freedom. Approval is socially desirable and a basic need of acceptance.

Without social context, nothing is rational. Rationalizing becomes very important. In other words, he can only justify the actions of the moment in terms of the moment. All ethics are useless. Thinking only wards off the future and is a means of escaping the past. Only the here and now exists. By the same token, there is no individual without the social, only individualizing. Individualizing has very little to do with being an individual or individualization. Individualizing is purely physical from the skin outward. It is a self that is momentary and situational.

Our hero's name is "Branded." His name or lack of is what he is. It doesn't matter if he did what he is accused of or not. The flesh, the man, is Branded.

Branded knows this, but still he fights. Why? Because although he has been stripped of the social power to name, he still knows he has the tools for naming. He still has language, that which makes us most human and that which enables naming. Language enables us to name our realities. We name the constructs and contexts that affect us most. Conversely, in the act of naming, we name things that we wish to exclude. The naming of our realities helps create our "selves." Branded still has the tools that provide him with the illusion that he can get back his name, although he lacks the social approval that must go with naming.

At an ontological level, our "name" is also our humanness. It stands for us. It differentiates us from things and others. Ernie is my identity to myself and other. It differentiates me from Lyz and Tony. It only assumes independence of ideas through its associations and difference. It merely demarcates my social identity on the social grid, but at the same time it gives me credence to name my world.

"Naming," then, is the self.

Branded, our hero, has ideas, but they won't matter until his own name is released from the shadow of social stigma. So our hero can try to construct an identity that is free, but he really can't have a complete identity until his name is cleared. He can only attempt to name. However, it is not attached to an identity, nor can it create one. Naming is self, not an identity.

In the latter half of the twentieth century, we came to overvalue the image of ourselves embodied in name only. We put more value in our naming ourselves. Maybe we do need our names more and more to differentiate us from and associate us with the exploding information that moves so easily and fast around the globe. In other words, we value names and naming to such a degree that they have become the reality. Naming is now greater than our individuality. Naming is how we individualize and possibly, as a result, deindividualize.

Naming and language have become our world. Language alone is our world; the world is the greatest illusion. It is no longer just a tool for describing or representing, but for referring to itself and its own uniqueness. Advertisements tell us to "Just do it" (Nike), "Just be" (Calvin Klein) in a way that refers to a personal language of the individual and the individual of personal language. We have become very cocky in our belief that language of the individual is all we need to be free, to the extent that we have become blind to the manipulation and control of political, social, and economic structures of large corporations. We are struggle in encouraged mock seriousness to create identities from mere language and, therefore, we ignore very real social constraints. At the same time, we are not unknowing of the social controls. We simply don't bother to understand social constraints because, we believe, we have no power over them and they are not the result of rational choice. But these social categories are the building blocks of identity.

The show *Branded* was on at a time when modernism was hemorrhaging and the struggle between identity and action or the self was paramount. The Vietnam War made American's question identity and action. Hippies, yippies, and others put great stock in differentiating themselves from others through their appearance. Even their issues were "dressed up" as art in their protest signs. As Stephen Stills wrote and sang, "Singing songs and carrying signs / Mostly say, 'Hooray for our side.'" Globalism was on the horizon, as witnessed in the student strikes around the world, especially evidenced by the situationists in France.

What if the program *Branded* were on today? If Branded were a postmodern citizen this is what would happen: The world would never know that Branded is not a coward. His identity is a relative truth. He fights for his name, and he can give that to himself. He can't be limited in the eyes of others. If he is, he merely changes his name. He doesn't struggle with the question of what is real and what is an identity or self.

So, does postmodernity free the new, transcendent Branded of all his struggles for identity? No. He is doomed. He is still a coward. He avoids knowing the "social" and his identity. He probes reality with his naming of it.

In the groundbreaking work, *Habits of the Heart*, Robert Bellah et al. (1985) argue that because individualism is at the heart of the American ideal, the definition of the self is important to the continuance of the society. They also argue "the self is the only main form of reality" (p. 144). They contend that many current problems go back to this concept of the self that has changed radically over the years. We are past a Romantic era in which a self is defined as a core person linked to everyone else. They agree that we are passing through and leaving an era in which each self is an autonomous choice maker who makes choices based on experiences of all types.

Bellah et al. fear that we are entering an era when feeling good replaces being good, an era in which there is no self, only a mask wearer. The authors believe that individuality is no longer defined as a collection of values, but as lifestyles. Self-expression has become dominant. The ability to change one's self without contradiction is of utmost importance.

Reality is currently false and decentered. It is false, on one level, because the self cannot be used to establish identity. It actually works the other way around; identity establishes the self or at least it has in the past. The self is also false because it only exists outside its own personality as a brand. The self is decentered, then, because it can live outside its own body in the contemporary mediated world. So, he rationalizes his identity and reduces it to the self. In other words, only his actions are what he believes to be his identity. He is constantly renewed, and yet schizophrenic.

In the end, we are all branded. We live in a social grid that is increasingly defined by our discourse about our social being vis-a-vis mass mass media institutions, content, and their relationship with us as subject. And a growing influence within that grid is the way we are depicted as subject of or affected by mass mass media. It is how we learn about how to think about ourselves. The new self is a teleself. The teleself (and we are all televiewers whether we watch television or not) is branded. This self turns a deaf ear to the social, believing that our identity is in his own ability to speak (no matter what he says). This provides us with the ultimate sense of free will or free choice, in this case the ultimate illusion.

By breaking with the past, the teleself's language, which is his mistaken identity, is free only to reference itself. He believes that his language is private and free. He further confuses this with free choice. His choices are "to be or not to be," to "be on or off," to "be himself or no one else." He is a digital being and his choices are reduced to binary choices: to believe or not to believe. This describes a generation that believes that the first opinion we should all have is whether to turn on the television. Or, when we don't agree with something, that we should take the choice of merely turning it off. Just disagreeing is not an opinion.

In such an environment, the self is defined not by values. One of the most resonating points that Bellah et al. make is that we live in an age when people talk about values but can't identify them. They argue that what is paramount is the ability to pick and choose values. "Choice is its own justification, because they define the true self" (p. 75). All of this fits the postmodern argument of the mutation of the self or the lack of self. The authors go further to fully support the poststructural notion that the language of the self precludes the physical or value defined self "insofar as they are limited to a language of radical individual autonomy, they cannot think about themselves or others except as arbitrary centers of volition. They cannot express the fullness of being that is actually theirs" (p. 81). Not only does language precede thought in the making of the self, but the authors argue that language itself limits the range of the self.

The teleself packages himself in the language of his relationship to the dominant medium. He is a model of what he wants to be. He is a pastiche—a free floating, nonreferential, self-referential model of himself. He is also a simulacrum—a better self than he could be. He can only be better if he frees himself from others' language. The attitude toward choice as digital and self-determined, however, leaves him vulnerable to what is real and what is the complete definition of the self—social structure, a social structure largely determined by or through our perceived relationship with television and in the mass media in general.

The idea of packaging the individual brings me to the way I use "branded" as a metaphor for the postmodern teleself. The postmodern viewer has transcended simple commodification of the self. As Bellah et al. note, "Now if selves are defined by their preferences, but those preferences are arbitrary, then each self constitutes a model universe, and there is finally no way to reconcile conflicting claims about what is good in itself" (p. 76). "A self free of absolute values can alter its behavior to adapt to others and to various social roles. It can play all of them as a game" (p. 77). The televiewer is not merely a product sold to the market. The teleself is a brand. His identity is a product that could be differentiated to a degree from other products, but his "self" covers it. The self is mere packaging that gives the illusion of product differentiation. This is the illusory power of names and naming.

The explosion of messages covers up the equally important implosion of diversity. As product packaging becomes more important and, consequently, diverse and prolific, the products inside become more alike. Just as the market is forced to make products more alike, so as not to offend, the teleself hides his identity so as not to offend. We hide behind or are hidden by our packaging. The "truth" is hidden and made relative, allowing the teleself to spend time on constructing a changeable packaging that sells for the moment. The teleself is not served by the mass media. He willingly delivers himself to them. He realizes that he is a package that is delivered by the mass media every day. He is quite aware of his role in the market.

Think about how someone may identify (and have long conversations about) with a fast food restaurant of choice—"I'm a McDonald's guy" or "I'm a Burger King person." I often joke with my students that on the day I turned thirty-five I could no longer drink Budwiser because I didn't fit the market segment. My point is not that we are frivolously defining ourselves (but we are). My point is that the hyperreal market feeds a hyperreal self and vice versa as inseparable parts. In an age of commodification, the parts could still be distinguished. Today, the self is a simulacrum of the late-capitalist market.

It is obvious that television is extreme, contradictory, and hyperreal. And it is equally obvious that everyone realizes this. However, it is part and parcel of late capitalism to use the extreme to cover the horrors of life. Late capitalism is the acceptance of the societal fragmentation, strife, and poverty of social Darwinism. We are not just unwillingly commodified anymore. We willfully seek to win in the market of brands at any expense or at anyone else's expense.

My thoughts are not necessarily new. Postmodernists have been talking for a long time about the lack or nonexistence of identity and the social construction of the self as a commodity. They cite many causes for our new nature that range from evolution to the cold war to capitalism in general. Some see the effect as a new age that rejects modernism and its materialism. Others see a new world of unimaginable technological advances that exult capitalism. Both are true and probably not worth arguing in isolation.

In short, I believe that we are a product of late capitalism (Jameson, 1988). What is postmodern is a late phase of hyper-commodification and fetishism. I believe that television gave us this new culture through its programs and advertising support. I also believe the evolutionary view that describes a human being relying on a new basic safety need—repetition as achieved through sameness and homogeneity.

My take on this is a bit different or at least broader. I believe that for us to speak of ourselves in a different way—that way being couched in a sense of safety in our language and creating life within situations rather than cultural contexts—we had to have been given a model for this discourse.

Therefore in this book, I will argue that the televiewer is the most recent construction of television itself, and, more importantly and precisely, how the mass media in general and television in particular has been presented in the discourse of research on television's effects. In other words, I believe that the person of the television age is the way he is—commodified, decentered, delusional, etc.—as a result of seeing own portrait painted by media effects studies. We have been fed a discursive regarding the mass media effects debate of how individuals and society relate to the mass media. I will eventually do this by describing the evolution of the discourse of mass media effects. By analyzing that same discourse more broadly I will show how the self has changed.

Chapter Two

Tools for Analysis: Social Psychology as History, the Social Grid, and Kuhn's Influence on Media Effects History

This chapter introduces the rationale for my overall approach, which is to look at the discourse of mass media effects research as a history and to further argue its relationship to the self. The first part of this chapter introduces Kenneth Gergen's (1973) "Social Psychology as History," which provides a rationale for examining scholarly studies in social psychology as history. This notion is a tailor-made approach for the present work. More specifically and fortuitously for the author, Gergen calls for the study of social psychology as history for the study the changing self. Foucault provides an extension of Gergen's work in that he speaks to the socio-cultural impact of research on the social grid, that everyday guide to cultural and social life.

Then we will turn to a thumbnail sketch of media effects history and discuss how the influence of Thomas Kuhn's (1963) way of telling history of a given discipline has strongly influenced the telling of our history.

Social Psychology as History

In 1981, Ralph Rosnow argued that a new paradigm of social psychology should be called for especially following the artifact, ethics, and relevance debates over the previous forty years. Critics of social psychology are concerned primarily with the core values of science, objectivity, and reliability. First, the experimental method of social psychology is "oblivious of how social phenomena were conditioned by developmental, ideological, or historical circumstances" (p. 73). The use of scientific methods assume that the phenomenon under study does not change in character. For example, if we were to study social identity, can we assume that the concept and its manifestations are unchanged over the years?

Second, it is important in science to assume stability, at least loosely so as to build some sort of evidence over time.

> Unlike the natural sciences, it deals with facts that are largely non repeatable and which fluctuate markedly over time. Principles of human interaction cannot readily be developed over time because the facts upon which they are based do not generally remain stable. Knowledge cannot accumulate in the usual scientific sense because such knowledge does not generally transcend its historical boundaries (p. 310).

The very idea that knowledge accumulates is debatable.

Rosnow credits Gergen with reviving the debate and arguing it to some strong conclusions and new directions. Gergen (1973), in a landmark work, argued that the methods of social psychology are scientific in character, but that the theories of social behavior are reflections of contemporary history. He believes that social psychology changes and shapes the actor's behavior; shapes the theorizing, values, and limits of the theorizing; and theorizes based on acquired disposition.

Let's look at the argument more closely. First, social psychology changes and shapes the actor's behavior. Gergen argued that the system of social psychology is a communication system in which the scientist indeed decodes behavior and transmits his interpretation to the populous in hopes of benefiting society.

> Most psychologists harbor the desire that psychological knowledge will have an impact on the society. Most of us are gratified when such knowledge can be utilized in beneficial ways. Indeed, for many social psychologists, commitment to the field importantly depends on the belief in the social utility of psychological knowledge. However, it is not generally assumed that such utilization will alter the character of causal relations in social interaction (p. 310).

What is important here is the argument that society is in touch with the science and the art of social psychology. The science, through its own status in our society, transmits truth about the respondents, which gives society the sense of self-evaluation (pardon the pun). The trap here is that the choice of topic was probably driven by its current status in contemporary history, thereby overemphasizing the importance of the phenomenon.

The art of social psychology is how it shapes us, or, if you will, paints a portrait of how we are and, like all art, might want to be. In a sense the knowledge gained has a liberating effect. Gergen writes, "the recipient of knowledge is thus provided with dual messages: Messages that dispassionately describe what appears to be, and those which subtly prescribe what is desirable" (p. 311). The process shows us ourselves, yet at the same time channels a view of ourselves within the possibilities of social science of the times and of the researcher. "So not only does the field operate to change (or sustain) interpretations, it also functions unwittingly as a moral and political advocate . . . The traditions most well known research, for example, discredits conformity, obedience, autonomy, and self-containment; cooperation, collaboration and emphatic integration of the other are also suppressed" (1996, p. 3).

These initial arguments do not suggest that social psychology is a biased waste of time, although many of Gergen's detractors saw his argument in that light. The point is to show that social psychology cannot and should not live in a vacuum. Otherwise it become a stage for self-fulfilling prophesies. By being self-reflexive, social psychology can build a better field of study and knowledge.

The arguments are not as shocking today as they once were. Hans-Georg Gadamer (1975) and Stanley Fish (1980), among others, have convincingly argued that all endeavors happen within interpretive communities and that in social science when the researcher is always a member of the subject of study, the interpretive community is left to interpret itself and the behaviors of the members. Kuhn's (1970) work also largely argued that communities of scientists are very aware of their membership and the structure of its paradigms.

This comes through in Gergen's second point that social psychology shapes theorizing. Topics chosen by the researcher are already significant and deemed significant but will not be scientifically significant until they have an impact on theory. Gergen argues that no particular problem changes a theory. Theories are "changed" because of societal changes. Therefore, we may believe that the study of a new phenomena may have shed new light on a theory when instead the phenomenon only reflects cultural change. Thus, theory is shaped and limited by culture.

He gives a good example in a later paper (1996). He tells the story of an experiment on self-esteem in which positive feedback by an interviewer increases the positive feelings of the subject-interviewee. He writes:

I argued that in order for others' feedback to affect one's level of self-esteem, this feedback would have to appear authentic. If one believed the feedback was insincere, not intended to be an accurate expression of feeling, then the feedback would have little effect. Indeed, I tested this hunch by running a group of subjects under the same conditions as above, with the exception of telling them that the interviewer would be practicing a set of interview techniques. The results confirmed my hypothesis. However in moments of repose, it also struck me that none of the feedback in any of the conditions was truly sincere; all of it was experimentally arranged. This meant that it was not what the interviewer actually did in the interchange that mattered, but the interpretation that was placed on it. Yet, if interpretations come and go across cultural history, and there is virtually no limit on the ways events can be interpreted, then what are we to make of these results? There was widespread belief at one time in people's souls, and in demonic possession; such interpretations are no longer favored. In the 16th century, states of melancholy were detected everywhere;

earlier in the present century, people suffered from "nervous breakdowns."
these interpretations are now little evidenced. My results seemed, then, to be reflections of the present cultural conditions (p. 2).

The most important part of Gergen's argument is the third point, that theory
is based on acquired disposition. He says that social psychologists are "engaged
in a systematic account of contemporary affairs" (p. 316). "Historians may look
back at such accounts to achieve a better understanding of life in the present era.
However, social psychologists of the future are likely to find little value in contemporary knowledge" (316). Again, we come back to the criticism that social
psychology is not cumulative. Rosnow reports that although some of Gergen's
assertions were refuted and that his notion of science is a bit rigid, "his assertion
that all things known are subject to historical change was an inescapable conclusion that could not be easily refuted" (p. 80).

Social psychology cannot only be read as an historical text; it is an excellent
history because it is systematic and exaggerated. It is systematic due to the stan-
dardization of the methods used. The telling of the history of any social psychology exaggerates the findings because that which is "significant" is usually
the only thing reported. It is also exaggerated, and this is especially true of mass
media effects, in that it is told using a Kuhnian narrative. The Kuhnian narrative
forces events or strings of events into paradigms and often stresses the sexy version of paradigm shifts that involve "eureka" or accidental moments and de-
emphasizes the nature of competition within paradigms. It must also be realized
that Kuhnian narratives force new ages "every week" instead of the hundreds of
years in which most "verifiable" shifts occur. This can be healthy for a field and
competition within it, but one must, as Gergen and Rosnow suggest, be a history
that is recognized as a socially constructed truth useful for self-reflection, not
facts to be built upon.

At the level of theory or paradigm formation, Gergen says that he was arguing for a principle that is argued in the natural science and that is that the purpose of natural science is to create dialogue. He delivers a reflexive challenge
which is the "process which calls attention to historical and culturally situated
character of taken-for-granted world which reflect on their potential for oppres-
sion and which open a space for other voices in the dialogue" (1996, p. 5). Reflexivity provokes dialogue, challenges to tradition, and new understandings.

After heralding a new approach, Gergen reminds the reader that the self is at
the center of the study of all psychological endeavors and that in order to start
anew we must return to the study of the self, "not as an internal emotionally
labeled self or a signified self, but a socially constructed self that is not made up
of love, hate, etc. but lovers and haters within a social context."

The present study takes Gergen up on his challenge to apply his method, to
do a rereading of the field and focus on how the field itself shaped the idea of
the self and was shaped by the contemporary view of the self.

Foucault and the Social Grid

The "history" presented later in this book is, simply speaking, a way of looking at how we have come to talk about mass media effects and, especially, its primary subject, the self. My purpose is to show how the self has been invented, further invented, reinvented, and mutated into a "self" through an evolving discourse. "Discourse," is the talk that is referred to here. More precisely, it is based on the rules of discussion of ideas, which includes who gets to discuss and what ideas are reified. "Reify," in this sense, means to concretize the ideas, a process I prefer to call "thingify." To "thingify" gives a sense of agreeing on a stable, unitary object or unit. Thingification, I believe, is necessary to the evolution of a set of ideas to become a discipline of study. So, on one level, I will cover the history of the study of mass media effects as it thingified its ideas as proprietary. Just as sociology thingified the masses or psychology thingified the psyche, communication thingified the self as its entree to disciplinary status. This process was necessary in the study of communication for it to have credibility and social clout.

At another level, I also hope to show how a discourse evolves. So far, all I have said is that the discourse of the field has evolved or mutated. If it were a completely random history, I would have nothing to write about here. However, there seem to be similarities between the human disciplines in how they have evolved as "sciences."

Foucault was the first to recognize and explain the evolution of the human disciplines as a product of discourse. Foucault's archaeologies (1970, 1972) must be examined here as the groundwork for my historical approach to the discipline with which this book is concerned. Foucault's archaeology of knowledge explains how disciplines develop a unitary, distinct discourse, necessary for the development of a vocabulary unique to the discipline.

In all of his works, Michel Foucault was interested in how man became an object of knowledge. He not only wanted to investigate how this came to be and why it might be a false science, he wanted to show how the nature of man is inseparable from language itself. In other words, if language precedes thought, then how can we describe the nature of man, i.e., how do we know when the tool is not that which it is making?

In *The Order of Things: An Archaeology of the Human Sciences*, Foucault (1972) takes on the role of archaeologist. As an archaeologist, he focuses on a single epoch. The archaeologist studies the formation of each individual epoch or what Foucault called episteme. An episteme is the "underground" grid of an epoch that allows thought to organize itself. The episteme limits the experience and search for knowledge. What where the understandings of the time? In Althusarian (with whom Foucault studied) terms, why where certain ideals taken for granted at certain time, or what was the force of taken-for-grantedness of the time?

Knowledge is the object that results from the discourse of the epoch. Knowledge, therefore, does not accumulate, but rather is tied directly to the discourse of the times. The discourse is the science or practice that gives form to the objects to be studied. The discourse of an epoch classifies what is to be studies and how it is studied.

Discursive regulations in any era or across epochs determine who speaks, under what conditions and what we speak about. The rules of knowledge formulated through discourse also formalize knowledge. Once knowledge is formalized, a construct of ontology emerges. Knowledge is a historical product of discursive interests and conditions. Construction of the human subject is contingent to the historical discourse.

Therefore, in order to truly examine history we must attempt to understand the discourse of the age. An archaeology of knowledge traces the rules and relations in knowledge production. It also frees us from being limited ourselves in our understanding of the history. History, then, is the act of tracing discourse within an epoch in order to describe the resultant objects or knowledge. Foucault's word to historians is that objects and relations about which we write in formalist history must be transcended. Foucault's point is to understand the discourse that is used to generate the objects and relations.

In order to illustrate what he meant by his archaeological approach, Foucault took on the history of the last five hundred years. In *The Order of Things*, Foucault analyzed the Renaissance, Classical, and modern epochs and their epistemes. In the Renaissance words and things were united in their resemblance. Things were explained through similarity, analogy, proximity, or attraction. The similarities among things could be recognized by man but their explanations were hidden by God. Hence, knowledge came through guessing and interpreting.

The Classical episteme is explained by the collapse of resemblance mainly from a new opposing force: difference. In the Classical epoch, classification (class) of knowledge created a demand for the creation of differences or for those differences to be noticed. Difference also demanded that classification have finite boundaries. Measurement and empirical verification became standards as standards themselves were in vogue. Words, as the primary measurement system of any classification system, then, had come to represent ideas directly. In philosophical terms, a correspondent theory of language arose—one word, one thing, perfectly matched. Instead of resemblance, the order of things was representation.

In the earlier epistemes, man guessed at what God hath wrought and then represented what God had made in him. In the modern episteme, man studies himself, not only as a subject, but as that from which all things come. Empirical life is the contents of one's body, social relations, his norms, and values. The rise of the human sciences (e.g., economics, biology, sociology, psychology) contribute to the need to establish underlying forces that describe surface regularities.

Language in the modern episteme is no longer the means to represent, but to be the very object of investigation. One can easily see this in the fathers of the modern age, Karl Marx and Sigmund Freud. Language is the mastery of the self or at least the illusion of the mastery of the self.

So where does that leave us?

An archaeological analysis of discourse can reveal more important concepts of the formation, local, and deployment of knowledge that inevitably construct human subjects: their assumed ontology, social positioning, practices, and relations (Luke, 1990). The archaeologist should be concerned with dismantling assumptions articulated by discourses. Foucault (1972) spoke about using "unities" as the starting point of investigation. Unities are created by discursive events that have defined the going assumptions of a field of knowledge. The unities are then interrogated from the standpoint of the external observer, never allowing oneself to accept the internal unities.

The unit of analysis in a Foucaultian analysis is effective statements, those statements that have been labeled as authoritative and that are regularly articulated and referenced. The analyst attempts to account for the discursive groupings of authoritative statements. Accordingly, the analysis should reveal positions and viewpoints of speakers and their institutions, who are then identified as authoritative, authorized, and privileged.

Discourse, in Foucault's case, is representative of the social. The discourse merely continues and codifies rules that delimit what can be said, who can say it, and when it can be said. This may go without saying, but discourse is not preceded by but is, concurrently, the social (Luke, 1990). This is important because it reminds us that the discourse of any time shows us more than just an arrangement of objects and ideas; at a deeper level, it reveals what the ontological beliefs were and more.

In examining discourse the interplay of two axes are examined. First, the code of any discourse conveys its rules and procedures. It lends an insight to rule-making and procedures. Second, the truth gives us an idea of the impact of authority upon the perceived truth of a message. In other words, truth in this case does not mean the inherent truthfulness of a message, but what authority gives the message truth, whether it be its source, institutional framework, etc.

This is very important and the point at which Foucault is at his best. Too often when something has reached print, it is assumed that it has met all criteria for truth. However, all criteria is only defined in terms of the "threshold of epistemologization" of the time. This is not to say that there is any deception or lack of rigor in true/false tests, but that only different assumptions guide the acceptability of findings as true. Therefore, at any given time validation procedures are always self-referential and self-justifying.

In order to break through the assumptions of truth, the analyst must dissect the dominant discourse and examine what Foucault calls the "discursive constellation" (1972, p. 66). The constellation is formed by: 1) why ideas are ordered as they are; 2) how institutions reflect the ideas and knowledge that they produce; 3) how the ideas are articulated; 4) what conditions are available for weakening dominant discourses and strengthening new ones; 5) individual or institutional authority available to reject old or new discourses; and 6) historical conditions for sanctioning authority.

All of these dimensions then are used to write a history that emphasizes three levels of discursive formation (Foucault, 1972). First, the surface of emergence appears. It is recognized when and from what conditions (social, political, cultural, etc.) objects and their resultant dominant discourses arise. Second, authorities of delimitation arise. Identifying authorities further insight into control of the discourse and for what reasons it is revealed. Lastly, the grid of specification becomes apparent. The grid is essentially the language used by authority to categorize their field. All operations are transformed to fit the grid and happen under the control of the grid. Where one fits in the grid or more simply, how one is labeled, is what they are and they act accordingly. Moreover, we are all defined by multiple grids. The more grids that we are influenced by fragments us into more and more pieces to the point where fragmentation itself works as a control.

The Telling of a Post-Kuhnian History

The history of media effects is a tightly packaged and almost universally agreed upon narrative. The narrative follows one suggested by Thomas Kuhn (1963). Kuhn argued that the history of science could be mapped out according to shifts in dominant paradigms which constitute a scientific era. The shifts themselves were established following the clash of competing paradigms or by some "eureka" moment of discovery.

Kuhn's work has become important to the telling of the histories of most intellectual fields. At the same time it is one of the most misused works. The word "paradigm" is uttered whenever someone wants to contain a dominant group of researchers or define their opposition. "Paradigm shift" is used to refer to laws new to a field. The word revolution is readily used to explain any finding that was not suspected. And, too often, revolutions are only thought to occur through some accident.

Although he admits that the word paradigm is broad, Kuhn specifically says that paradigms are defined through conflict and by their laws, theories, methods, application, and instrumentation. All are needed together to make up a paradigm and act as a guide to what is acceptable within a paradigm. A change or use of multiple approaches within one of the parts of a paradigm does not make for a revolution. For example, the change of methods in a paradigm does not constitute a shift or create a revolution. As a matter of fact, Kuhn writes that within most healthy paradigms multiple methods are used. For example, in math both quantitative and qualitative approaches are used. One is used to articulate the other.

The internal dialogue within a strong discipline can also create a paradigm. Kuhn says that all strong paradigms are always esoteric. The discourse of the field builds a cant that not only bolsters professional lines drawn in the sand but creates a stronger discourse with specific agreements on the terms used within a field or discipline. Much of Edward O. Wilson's book, *Consilience* (1999), is devoted to arguing that a discipline needs to develop its own vocabulary or agreed upon terms. He argues that although the social sciences are just as rigorous and available as the natural sciences, they will never be able to gain the same status until they develop a vocabulary and leave bickering over language behind. Of course, these kinds of arguments are difficult to apply because of the problems of being so self-conscious of language. Such self-consciousness leads to a disciplinary Esperanto. When language is forced on people it creates a false sense of security and also creates illusions of paradigm shifts.

Most of the histories that apply Kuhnian notions, at least in the social sciences, also seem to believe that some day conflict will not be necessary and that a perfect paradigm will be achieved. This belief creates greater dissatisfaction with the field and a feeling of underachievement. Kuhn tells us that the pulse of a paradigm is conflict and the feeling that it can still be attacked. Paradigms are never stable. It is their nature to be self-critical. "Paradigms promise success but need more examples" (p. 23).

Kuhn's influence has certainly made most disciplines rewrite their histories for better or worse. But in the case of the discipline of mass communication, Kuhn's influence has been unprecedented and generally unquestioned. This is because the history of mass communication was one of the first histories of a discipline to be told after Kuhn published his work. The telling of a Kuhnian history was not only contemporary to the history of mass media effects, but without a doubt so in vogue to the point that the telling was rarely questioned. This can be recognized merely by noticing the number of supposed paradigm shifts in a history that is less than a century old. Most much older disciplines have paradigm shifts more rarely in the telling of their histories.

The historical discourse will be analyzed later, but for now a sketch of the history is warranted. James Carey (1996, 22) wrote that the history of media effects can be reduced

to something like this. Mass communication research began in the years surrounding World War I as a response to a widespread fear of propaganda; wartime propaganda by the major military powers, peacetime propaganda by organized interests, particularly the modern corporation and the business class. The fear of propaganda was fueled by the spread and increasing sophistication of advertising and public relations, but the indictment of these practices moved from the arena of news and public affairs across the landscape of mass-produced culture and entertainment. If the cognitive and attitudinal life of citizens was under assault of propaganda, the moral, appreciative, and affective life of children (and the child in all of us) was similarly assaulted by a banal and pernicious system of cultural production emanating from massive, concentrated institutions. As the "jazz age" turned into the Great Depression, the fears of propaganda and the media were confirmed by mass movements in politics and culture typical of the period and by a series of specific and startling events of which Orson Welles' radio broadcast "War of the Worlds" stood as an archetype. In the standard history, this random assortment of fears, alarms, jeremiads, political pronouncements, and a few pieces of empirical research were collapsed into the "hypodermic-needle model" or "bullet theory" or "model of unlimited effects" of the mass media, for they converged on a common conclusion: The media collectively, but in particular the newer, illiterate media of radio and film, possessed extraordinary power to shape the beliefs and conduct of ordinary men and women.

Carey then goes on to say that this paradigm had no real theoretical or empirical support. The first paradigm was used as a point of departure, but not one to build upon but one to tear down. This is not suprising. What else would one do if influenced by a Kuhnian history? One must, if we are going to have a history find some paradigm to replace. One paradigm does not make a history. Obviously, the simple initial paradigm is so constructed to be very easily destroyed so as to be replaced by another paradigm and, hence, have a history-in-the-making and a ready-made discipline.

Carey continues:

> beginning in the late 1930s and progressively throughout the 1940s, a body of empirically sophisticated and theoretically grounded research began to appear . . . that decisively cut against the hypodermic-needle model of media effects. What was discovered, almost fortuitously it seems, was a bizarre situation in which there were causes without effects, stimuli without responses . . . investigators produced evidence that the content or intentions were rarely tied to effects or consequences. What was also discovered, in the standard rendition, was that individuals, the members of the audience, were protected . . . by predispositions or mediating factors . . . [M]edia propaganda and mass culture were held at bay by an invisible shield erected by a universally resistant psyche and a universally present network of social groups (23).

Thus the second paradigm known as limited effects was born and so was a discipline. Whether it's the first, second, or not a paradigm at all is not the issue here. The point is that the history of the discipline is uncontested. This is not to say that I am arguing for this view of the history; I am merely trying to state the facts.

For the purpose of discussion, I will rely on the "established" history of mass media effects (Bryant and Thompson, 2002). As in any discipline there has been rewriting and revision of the history. The point here is not to deconstruct history but to give a profile of the "learned history," that which has probably had the greatest social impact. In other words, the established history, right or wrong, is akin to an outline of a standardized textbook, one whose power cannot be denied or repressed.

The established history of media effects can be divided into four eras or shifts in the paradigm. The first era is defined by the magic bullet model, from about 1920 to 1945. The second era is the limited effects model, 1945-1970, followed by a strengthening of the effects model during the moderate effects stage, 1960-1985. Presently, it may be argued that strong effects reside, although not the same kind of strong effects as put forth in the magic bullet era (See Figure 2.1).

Media Effects Model

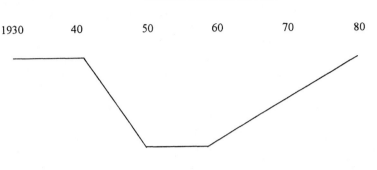

| 1930 | 40 | 50 | 60 | 70 | 80 |

Bullet Theory
Payne Fund Studies

Limited Effects
"Why We Fight"
Studies
Yale Group

Mounting Evidence
Two-Step Flow-1955
Diffusion Of Innovation-1962
Cultivation Hypothesis-1970
Agenda Setting-1972

Figure 2.1.

Tensions and the Creation of Paradigm Shifts

Influenced by Kuhn's idea that science progresses through paradigmatic competition, shifts in the discipline are often attributed to shifts in theatrical insight. However, I will show that the tensions are primarily methodological differences at best and that what really is changing greatly is the global notion of the self. Therefore, Kuhn has been misapplied in this case.

Theories change and become slightly more powerful. But instead of being what we usually only think of as better, more powerful theories, they are also reflections of what has changed in the nature of the more recent self. Simply put, the discipline's shifts in theories is less attributable to the theories themselves than to the changing nature of the self.

Most works on the history of the discipline of communication are written from one of two broad perspectives. Many works follow the "dominant paradigm" of mass media effects (e.g., Bryant and Thompson, 2002; Dennis and Wartella, 1996; Rogers, 1994). Others follow the mass media studies "paradigm" (e.g., Czitrom, 1982). Very few attempt to tackle both at the same time. Lowery and DeFleur (1988) make the best attempt at it.

Although the two approaches have been around from the beginning, they really weren't recognized as "opposing" perspectives until the 1960s. In her book *Electronic Hearth*, Cecilia Tichi (1991) writes about the development of opposing perspectives. She shows how they arose from larger social questions rather than academic arguments. In her book she examines the place of television within American family. She describes changes in the relationship between individuals and television over time. In the 1950s and '60s, amidst the rhetoric of individualism, to watch television alone was to abandon the family, to be a loner. The portable television, even if not portable, symbolized a new individual, one who could be alone with the television. The technology promoted escape from the family for just a little while. Of course, this image points to the male. In any case, this metaphor is one of a viewer taking control of the situation.

Tichi argues (a la Baudrillard) how our sense of individualism affected our relationship with television. Freedom to be an individual in America became equated with desire for the product, to "actualize the self in consumption, each on his own," and that personal liberty has thus taken the form of individuals' acquisition of products and services, including television receivers and programs.

The "new" viewer spurred on the public's interest in human/media relationships. Social scientists had already been studying the effects of modern mass media. Television opened up an entirely new world for social scientists. Researchers in communication, sociology, English, rhetoric, anthropology, and psychology began studying more intensely the relationship between the viewer and the television.

As the arguments became more public, two ways of constructing and studying the viewer quickly emerged. Tichi talks about the two irreconcilable versions of the viewer constructed by researchers. One is the stupefied addict, the second a figure stimulated by and actively engaged with the images on the screen (p. 104). The stupefied addict is the product of mass media effects. The stimulated figure is the construction of mass media studies.

The two schools of thought are set in opposition in the academic discourse. Media effects constructs a more passive viewer. Media effects studies use standard scientific measurement techniques through surveys and experiments. Media effects is known by the public through the reported results of violence studies and most studies on children and television.

Media studies is the alternative or opposing "paradigm." It has always been posited as a weaker view, probably because it is socially less desirable in a scientific, capitalistic society. Media studies constructs a more active viewer within a cultural setting. Their methods of observation and measurement allow the painting of larger landscapes that include the culture of the viewer softening the starkness of the lone viewer.

The two views obviously differ in their means of study. The means seemingly come to different ends. On the surface this is true. However, as will be shown, the ends or construction of the viewer are not different in an ontological sense.

The two views are often said to struggle over paradigmatic rights, to present two different worldviews. However, there have been no true paradigmatic challenges to the way we perceive the viewer. The real paradigm shifts, if any, are in the way the nature of the self has changed in the last decades. Theory follows practice in this sense, as much as theory helps construct and solidify the self in society. If anything has been accomplished in the struggle between the two views it has been that both have progressed because of the competition. The two schools have been integrated to form a new modified view. In other words, the two schools have forced a good dialogue that for the most part has served to promote integrative thinking, not separation.

Although these views are always presented in conflict, I believe they are not. They are, as Tichi says, irreconcilable. Tichi presents the dominant way of examining the struggle between the effects and studies paradigms. All constructions for the viewer are right and parallel, interacting with one another (in the same way that theory interacts with philosophy). More specifically, the views interact with a changing nature of the self. Both are valid ways of seeing that depend on the nature and inclusiveness of the question. The approaches act together in enforcing a discourse about the viewer. They are not opposing paradigms—that is what this chapter, at the theoretical level, is about.

The so-called effects school has been the dominant paradigm in mass media research. Although it is based on many wrong-headed assumptions, its centrality makes it right. Because it is central to all arguments, pro and con, it is the focus of not only mass media studies but more importantly the public discourse. In our market driven society, all ideas about mass media and society start and end with the effects paradigm.

Because it is central and so public (probably more than any other contemporary academic endeavor), it has remained relatively simple, positivistic, and progressivist. Parsimony drives the mass media effects paradigm. It continues, no matter its trappings, to focus on the individual as agency, which in the American individualistic culture is much easier to understand.

Media effects has remained blindly progressivist. Despite the heralding of sea changes in the paradigm, the changes tend to remain within the paradigm. Its challengers have tended to merely support the assumptions of the effects school. Alternative or rival paradigms have been little more than methodological challenges. They all lack challenges to the theoretical structures, let alone ontological or epistemological structures.

For example, the uses and gratifications approach supposedly challenged the effects paradigm. Uses and gratifications touted a new method that transformed the viewer from an inactive to active viewer. Analyses focused on the individual viewer as active chooser and interpreter of messages. In the end, however, the viewer was still ontologically the same—someone who is affected by messages that come from institutional sources.

The two approaches of the viewer inhabit separate, opposed worlds of representation. The viewer is active at his level of interaction. It may be argued that at some level—e.g., ideological, politically—the viewer is not active. I might add that the viewer is active with television content, but passive about his relationship with the television.

Tichi talks about the struggles between two very real, tenacious groups: mass media studies and mass media effects. Their tussle alone has hastened the development of the discipline of communication. Although the fight is real, sometimes the assumed differences between the groups are overstated. The most obvious is that mass media studies is more qualitative, which suggests a sense of attention to social interpretation and orientation, and cultural-historical grounding. These are true, but they imply an orientation of theory that is opposed to empirical study. Media effects is often argued to be quantitative. By default this has deemed it empirical, not only because of the methodologies used but because of its positioning by its opposition. It also is true that mass media effects has embraced the label of empiricism. It would be stupid not to in an age that glorifies science.

The point of my analysis, however, is not to point out the self-deception that has gone on in the social science of communication, but to the description of the audience itself as it has been created in the methods (ostensibly, the theory) of the viewer. The purely methodological shifts in the effects paradigm have created a viewer who believes that he has full control and choice. This work asks how has the research on the viewer affected his perception of himself?

Formative Models

The primary reason that mass media effects and mass media studies are similar is that they both are posited from the same communication models. Whether used to make arguments based on them or against their assumptions, the models have had great impact. The models, often called transmissions models, are simple, point to point, linear models. Because they are easily visualized, the models biggest impact has been on the conceptualization of empirical research.

There are three versions of the general communication model: 1) the propaganda model, 2) the information model, and 3) cybernetics. The first model, devised by Harold Lasswell (1926), was used to introduce the concept of propaganda. More precisely, the model illustrates the movement of a message from a source through to its receiver and effect. The model is usually illustrated in this way: Who—Says What—To Whom—Through What Channel—With What Effect.

This model has all of the basic characteristics of a transmission model. Lasswell's model of message transmission directs a message from one person or entity to another. Notice that the entity precedes the idea. The idea or speech act is constructed as someone says it. It does not exist in the "who." What is said constitutes a message that is transmitted through some form. This concept is linear; one communicator to another through a non recursive channel. The assumption that this is some effect supports a property common to all transmission models. Therefore, we can also call transmission models behaviorist in orientation. It is behaviorist in that it assumes not only an effect but effects that are uniform across receivers (i.e., I am affected the same way you are affected and so on).

The properties of linearity are continued in the model that has been most influential across all contexts of communication studies (Fiske, 1982; Richie, 1986), the information model (Weaver, 1949). Warren Weaver applied the model using a paper published by Shannon (1948) a year earlier. The model was originally created to illustrate the properties of technical, electronic communication. Shannon was working on information transmission using binary code.

Weaver adapted the problems of the paper to human communication questions: How accurately can the symbols of communication be transmitted? How precisely do the transmitted symbols convey the desired meaning? How effectively does the received meaning affect conduct in the desired way?

These were the main questions and the bulk of the work was based on these theories that have fathered the digital age. The model used to illustrate how information travels from a source to a destination looked like this: Sender—>Encode—>Channel—>Decode—>Destination. It is read: Sender Encodes a Message through a Channel, the Message that is Decoded at a Destination. In his history of the discipline, Everett Rogers (1994) writes:

> Shannon's one-way model of the communication act helped launch the academic field of communication study (Rogers and Kincaid 1981, p. 33). More than any other theoretical conceptualization, it served as the paradigm for communication study, providing a single, easily understandable specification of the main components in the communication act: source, message, channel, receiver. Thus, communication investigations of the communication act could identify source variables (such as credibility), message variables (like the use of fear appeals), channel variables (such as mass media versus interpersonal channels), and receiver variables (like the persuadability of individuals). Dependent variables in communication research measured effects, such as knowledge change on the part of receivers, attitude change (persuasion), and overt behavior change like voting for a candidate or purchasing a new product.

The information model also shares the shortcomings of propaganda model. The information model assumes one direction, effects of a message, and uniformity of effects. Neither the propaganda nor the information model includes a conceptualization of reaction to the message (obviously they wouldn't, if direct, strong, and uniform effects are assumed).

The advantages of the model are also its problems: simplicity, generalizability, and quantifiability. The model's simplicity makes it transferable to many situations outside the intended purposes. Rogers (1994) writes:

> Thus, it seemed facile to translate the Shannon (1949) model of communication into a general classificatory scheme for the variables included in communication research. The apparent simplicity of the model made it attractive to communication scholars. Notice, however, that the dependent variables are communication effects on the part of the receiver, a development that went beyond Shannon's original focus on channel capacity as the dependent variable (p. 438).

At the same time, the model may not fit or oversimplify communicative situations, especially in the realm of mass communication. The models generalizability is derived from its parsimony. But again it may fail in certain contexts. For example, content and its readership are assumed to be uniform. This assumption also leads to ends-type thinking or instrumentality, in which the desired results are based on previous notions of what a subject is and how it uses objects. Quantifiability is key to survival in our age. Quantifiability is given more attention in our age of science. The field of communication has survived and flourished because of its emphasis on quantifiability. However, some relationships, depending on the question, are better answered critically. Also, some relationships that may be quantifiable are too difficult to understand especially when too many variables are in the mix.

There were attempts to "open" the systems model in Weaver's definition of communication: "all procedures by which one mind might affect another" (Weaver, 1949, p. 4). Weaver went on to explain the nature of noise in the human communication process. He named two types of physical noise in a channel. Environmental noise included noise from outside the channel. Semantic noise included any type of interference within the encoding or decoding system. In this way, Weaver attempted to address the language process, albeit very broadly.

In his attempt to "humanize" the model, however, great liberties were forced upon the human communication process. The model reduces communication to information processing or to a simple act of transmission. There is no room in the model for human terms, such as message, meaning, understanding, etc. At least in the Lasswell model "usage" alluded to a human process.

At the same time that Shannon and Weaver were uncovering the secrets of the binary information system, Norbert Wiener was working on similar projects at MIT. Wiener was very sensitive, however, to the effects of environment on the transmission of messages (actually, before that, missiles).

In *Cybernetics: Communication and Control in Animals and Machines* (1961) and *The Human Use of Human Beings* (1954), Wiener wrote of the importance of understanding the environment in which a system operates and, most importantly, the link between the two, called feedback. Wiener saw feedback as the most important part of the communication process. It might be said that feedback is the primary message link that formulated all understanding of the main message system. Feedback is a particular type of communication message flow, in that the information conveyed describes the system's performance at a previous point in time to itself. In other words, all of what we have determined to this point to be communication is really a result of some reaction to something that happened in the environmental system. We are reacting to feedback at all times.

Therefore, communication is the result of the overall regulatory system, which could be our physical environment, our meeting place, who we are meeting, etc. Rogers (1994) says:

> Cybernetics implies a dynamic, precessual view of behavior over time. Cybernetics assumes that the control of a system lies mainly within the system itself. The results of a system's own actions provide new information by which it modifies its subsequent behavior. Thus, the system learns from itself. Information about changes in the environment affect the system only as they necessitate adjustment to feedback. However, this idea seemed to get lost in the discourse about the communication model, the dominance of the information model, emphasis on communication as a discipline and, certainly, when social scientists combined the best of both the information and cybernetic models (p. 406).

Wiener's cybernetics has not been widely or directly used in communication research. It is mainly known for its additions or reconceptualizations of the information model. First, feedback was added to the information model. Communication scholars like David Berlo (1960) sought to conceptualize a components model of the communication act as a process over time.

Schramm's (1964) work is the best known of the attempts to combine the ideas and expand the model to include human communication. Schramm developed a series of models that started by including the feedback link in the model. Knowing that feedback is as important in the communication process as the primary message link and realizing that linearity is a weakness in the model, Schramm created a circular model with communicator as both senders and receivers sending messages to one another in a neverending loop. The model was important in revealing problems with existing model. However, it came to only reinforce the inadequacies of the information model. In the end, effects and uniform effects are still difficult to avoid imagining. And the model almost single-handedly obliterated the subtleties of cybernetics and the primary importance of feedback.

Second, "the one-way conception of human communication was later modified further in communication models of convergence based on information exchange among two or more participants." Berlo's (1977) incorporation of feedback into the communication process was a step in this direction. Everett Rogers and D. Lawrence Kincaid (1981, p. 37-75) depicted communication as a process in which individuals act as "transceivers," both transmitting and receiving information in order to reach common understanding. "Increasingly, communication has been viewed in communication models as a process, rather than as an act, a movement away from Shannon's linear model of communication" (Rogers, 1994, p. 438).

In the end, the problem may not be with a model, but with models in general. Their visual orientation may be too limited for a the complex process of communication, which is hyperdimensional or lacks dimensionality. Or like any language, its direction may dictate primary and secondary position in its conceptualization.

The broad legacy of these models has been an emphasis on a human engineering approach to communication. Weaver spoke of the study of communication as "concerned with . . . meaning conveyed . . . to the desired conduct" (p. 5). "In engineering, interpretation or understanding has no meaning apart from control" (Ritchie, 1986, p. 284).

More specifically, the approach had been reduced to simple behaviorism. Alfred Smith (1966, p. 8) wrote, "We particularly need empirical data when using electronic theories as points of departure for human theories because translations from one theory to the other are otherwise questionable analogies." The effectiveness of messages in the engineering approach are judged on acceptance. "If an advertiser sends a signal specifying 'buy Sudso Soap' . . . then the only meaningful question is 'does the receiver buy the soap?'" The idea that an individual might understand a message but choose to disregard it, or that a message might, as the Mona Lisa, have enduring value precisely because it calls for an ambiguous or open-ended interpretation, has no place in an engineering model. The semantic aspects are irrelevant in the engineering approach.

The development of communication models and research have not shed the chains of the simple communication models. Even those that have been deemed alternative or come from outside the field are forced to come to terms with and speak to the communication model. This has not only limited the scope of communication research but, more importantly for this work, has limited descriptions of the viewer to those based on an engineering approach, which have engineered the viewer.

The following, then, is a description of the discourse on mass media effects. The purpose is to show several interactions. At one level I describe of the progress within each school of thought. Their interactions between one another needs to be covered to give any credence to each school's history. At another level, I want to show how the development of the field has interacted with the models just described. In the end, I wish to show that through these interactions the discipline has painted a very strong, singular picture of the viewer, that both mirrors and strengthens the branded self.

Oppositional Paradigms

If paradigm shifts do occur, then an opposing paradigm at least exists or may have caused the shift. The same is true here. The discourse between the opposing perspectives looks something like this:

Opposing Paradigms

Media Effects	Media Studies
1) Magic Bullet	Symbolic Interactionist
2) Limited Effects	Marxist/Critical
3) Moderate Effects	Uses and Gratifications
4) Strong Cognitive Effects	Cultural Theory

Figure 2.2.

In this model each era has not replaced the last as time passes. They are not epochs. All are still in use. This is often referred to the previous era being "folded into the next." For example, symbolic interactionism has been revived many times and has mutated in other forms and within new theories at various times.

I also wish to show that in the practice of theory there have been no real paradigmatic shifts or oppositions in the development of the construction of the view/self. The perceived oppositions or shifts in a paradigm are real at the methodological level, but not at a level of knowledge. What we have learned about is a general shift in the notion of the self in our society and, at the same time, we have constructed an even more narrow view of the postmodern self. Therefore, my purpose is to show that the social scientists have correctly, for the most part, analyzed our society from the times of early social scientific practice, but more importantly, I hope to show that their practice has had a great effect on the construction of the social discourse, in this case the construction of the viewer.

Chapter Three

The Passive Self

In the remaining chapters, I will go through each paradigm in terms of themselves and their oppositions. The point is to argue that what the struggle has really done is to describe and enforce the view of the viewer as self, as represented in the column to the far right (see Figure 3.1).

Dominant Paradigms and the Related Self

	Media Effects	Media Studies	Self
1)	Magic Bullet	Symbolic Interactionist	Passive
2)	Limited Effects	Marxist/Critical	Active
3)	Moderate Effects	Uses and Gratifications	Commodified
4)	Strong Cognitive Effects	Cultural Theory	Teleself

Figure 3.1.

The importance of showing this, as I have stated elsewhere, is that I believe that the viewer is the self, that at the core of our description of a postmodern self is the construction of the self as viewer.

As I argued in the last chapter, social scientists are increasingly more powerful in our postmodern environment in setting the public discourse. With that said, the present work advances a singular model of the evolution of the construction of the viewer. Now that the archaeological site has been chosen and justified, I will employ the tools outlined by Jean Baudrillard as the mutation of the sign. My model, with shifts from passive, active, commodified, and the teleself, is supported by his stages of counterfeit, production, simulation, and simulacrum.

Mutation of the Sign

In *The System of Objects*, Baudrillard argues that in the production of meaning and reproducing the code (that which is ideologically right), we have come to value the simulation of meaning over the code. In addition, we have come to value the perfection of simulation until we no longer want the real. We only want the simulacrum. We don't want nature: we want parks. We don't value living as much as the look of health, which can be bought. We don't want foreign culture; we want Disneyland.

In *Simulations*, Baudrillard develops a framework that can be used to show how our signs have mutated to include such odd representations. The project at hand must be described at greater length. Baudrillard's (1983b) method addresses the postmodern subversion of signs from a cultural, evolutionary point-of-view. Baudrillard believes that all signs have historically "mutated" through three phases: 1) counterfeit; 2) production; and 3) simulation. The counterfeit was the dominant scheme of the period from the Renaissance to the Industrial Revolution. Production is the dominant scheme in the industrial era. Simulation is the current mutation. Mutated means that subsequent phases do not replace previous phases, they contain and add to them. Therefore, we live in an era in which all possible interpretations of the world are in place.

The first order of the sign, the counterfeit, mirrored that which it represented. Counterfeits were limited in number (like that which it represented) and, therefore, had to be clear and "anything but arbitrary" (p. 84). The primary function of the counterfeit was to pass value from one class to another. To hold the sign represented an upward transcendence of class. Concurrently, counterfeits enforced class structures in their unequivocal reference to status and their production by the bourgeoisie. For example, an advertisement or facsimile copy of a status symbol, such as a Rolex watch, transmits its class referent. It reminds the user that they do not belong to the class that can own the Rolex and are of a class that prizes fakes. This still holds true today. All signs are, to some degree, a reminder of the social class system.

The second order of signs references the boundless possibilities of mass production. The "energetic economic myth proper to modernity." (p. 97) is the industrial purpose for the sign. It conveys the modern myth of scientific production. The value of the industrial sign was no longer only in its referential value but in its commercial value vis-a-vis other signs and is "conceived from the point-of-view of [its] very reproducibility" (p. 100). Buying into the competition of signs and choosing a sign gave a stronger sense of belonging to industrial progress than holding a single counterfeit. For example, the multiplicity of ads or copies of the Rolex reminds us of the gifts of industrialization.

The postmodern sign is a simulation in spite of the reality. It no longer has to signify just class or social reality. It signifies a relativistic reality—a reality held only by the individual(istic) consumer. The sign comes to signify the hyperreality of the cybernetic relationship between the market and consumer (Baudrillard, 1981). In other words, the consumer believes that he/she is the sender of a message ("I get what I want") and the sign represents not a message but feedback (Sarup, 1993). Consumers come to believe that the sign is their own creation. The sign must tactfully allow the consumer to believe that he/she is in complete control of the sign. "The receiver/consumer is the god who guarantees that the [mass media content] 'works' or has 'meaning.' Only the recipient of the message can guarantee that the language . . . is spoken well" (Poster, 1990, p. 67).

The value of the sign is, therefore, in its emotional interaction with the consumer (I will continue to use the term "consumer" for the sake of convention and organization, although it implies a sense of receiver of messages instead of sender, which is the illusion). Poster (1990) describes Baudrillard's position on mass media effects in terms of advertising:

> Baudrillard's argument is not that people "believe" the ad; that itself would assume a representational logic, one subject to cause-effect analysis (how many people bought the product because they saw the ad). Nor is his argument based on irrational manipulation; the ad works on the unconscious of the viewer, subliminally hypnotizing the viewer to buy the product. . . . Instead Baudrillard sets his argument in linguistic terms: the ad shapes a new language, a new set of meanings (floor wax/romance) which everyone speaks or better which speaks everyone (p. 58).

Even more seductive is that collecting (knowing) signs gives the consumer more emotional feedback or the feeling of belonging to a world of free choices. The new consumer fetishism is the stockpiling of repetitious signs. The consumer "freely" collects signs that signify the self. As they are caught up in a play of repetitive images, the consumer world becomes relative and external to "reality." As in any evolutionary system, sameness and lack of reference points create a greater level of comfort with day to day existence (Baudrillard, 1983a).

This behavior is reinforced by the market economy. Since information has become the key to moving product, information has been given precedence over product itself. To limit the probable confusion in the market, distinction is given to information, while products are made to fit simple, broad, and arbitrary categories. Once classified, products become more and more alike. The consumer is not concerned with product limitations since he or she equates the proliferation of information with the real product choice.

Both McLuhan (1964) and Baudrillard (1983a) have spoken about the explosion of information and implosion (Best and Kellner, 1991) of real choice. Baudrillard describes this contradiction as a major social control device of late capitalism. He argues that implosion is a result of the erasing of the distinctions between communities, disciplines, politics, signs, etc. Everything is reduced to information. Baudrillard might agree that as perceived choice expands in the form of competing signs, real choice shrinks. Wants take precedence over and obscure any needs (Baudrillard, 1983a). "We are now living in an era of implosion, of the collapse of previous differences, distinctions, and hierarchies. There has been a transformation from stable referents to 'floating signifiers'" (Sarup, 1993, p. 167). This describes the end of the consumer society and industrialization and the beginning of a postmodern, postindustrial era.

In the end, product value is measured by its exposure and recognizability, not by its own use- or exchange value. The actual products themselves can become more similar as long as an illusion of choice is constructed by and for the consumer through the mass media. This brings us full circle back to a gluttonous consumer who emotionally envisions him or herself as the prime mover in the explosion of information. In such an environment, the consumer wants to express him or herself in the increasingly visible explosion of brand information. Ultimately, the consumer identifies himself as being as unique as a brand (which underneath is not very unique).

In other words, what color is a chameleon in a mirror? In the past the chameleon would have responded to the medium itself and become silver. Today, the chameleon is so familiar with the medium that it looks to the medium for a model of itself. The chameleon becomes colorless, less truthful to itself, but at the same time believes it has greater choice in the matter.

Madan Sarup (1993) refers to this production of consumer as the illusion of "privatized individuals" (p. 165). What the market "does to you is what you do to yourself and the way it does this is by being about itself" (Wagner, 1995, p. 61). "People are about it in somewhat the same way as the product is about it and it is the contingency of each to the other that the ad performs or replaces" (p. 60). In short, the market now produces consumers at the consumers' expense and compliance.

Jacques Attali (1989) uses Baudrillard's three mutations in his work. I will describe them here to illustrate the utility of Baudrillard's work in the analysis of a cultural phenomenon, in this case the political economy of music. First, Attali shows how signs, in his case music, can be used to examine historical and cultural phenomena as both causes (structuring) and results (structured) of the sign. This follows the logic of a more traditional structuralism. He writes specifically about the evolution of the "music code" (p. 5). He believes that sound has fashioned society more than any other code, e.g., color or form. Sound is uniquely versatile. Its clamor, melody, dissonance, and harmony have powerful effects of repression, control, restraint, etc. "All music, any organization of sounds is then a tool for the creation or consolidation of community, of a totality. It is what links a power center to its subjects, and thus . . . is an attribute of power in all of its forms" (p. 6).

Second, Attali melds critical and postmodern theory. He uses Baudrillard's phases to guide shifts in the political economy of music. At the same time, Attali strengthens and verifies some of Baudrillard's ideas. Attali argues that the music code has been transformed through three dominant zones: sacrificing, representing, and repeating. The first of Attali's zones, "sacrificing," describes the development of the music code in the West as the conscious control of noise cause people to forget the violent nature of birth and death. Whomever (usually royalty, court music) controlled the code held the knowledge to control the din of death and, therefore, controlled the community. Performers were kept from controlling the code by their imposed ambiguous job descriptions—i.e., they were organized as disorganized musicians-shamans-doctors-vagabonds. Audiences believed that the powers knew what was good for them. "Believers" (p. 19) sacrificed themselves to the code. The result was a distinction between high and low cultural forms of the "art." "Believers" could counterfeit the art of the royalty by listening to their music or they could create their own music. Paradoxically, in either case, both court and folk music acted as a reminder of class position.

Division and specialization of labor erased these controls. As capitalism grew, the contradictions of this zone became more contentious. Attali notes the contradiction that created a new zone: "No organized society can exist without structuring differences at its core. No market economy can develop without erasing those differences in mass production" (p. 6). The musician cast off his old master but was channeled forever as a commodity. In other words, as the artist and audiences broke down the controls over art by the elite, they gave in to new structural controls—in this case, market controls. Music ultimately came under control of the soul that created it but, simultaneously, music had to become a commodity. At least part of the musician's "self" had to become marketable.

The result was "representing," Attali's second zone of the political economy of music code. Massification or industrialization of the art became essential to maintain control over one's own art. Historically, concessions were granted in copyright permissions and concomitant recognition of artists and their art. These artistic freedoms came with more subtle controls. The artist became more responsible for the capital of operations, for mass production (to achieve economies of scale), and for industrialization (to cut expenses) of his art.

More music was forced to harmonize with the larger community. Mass production became "deafening" as the market drove the artist to conform to its repetitive codes. "Popularizing" of music led to the last full zone: "repeating." Repetition became the key for success, but also led to inevitable failure. The art and artist were reduced to technique and technicians, respectively. Technologies of repetition and reproduction were now in the hand of the audience who control (re)creation. "More of the same" is the key; more of the same sounds and more for the same tired, stereotypical categories. The goal became to organize the audience in easily recognizable and stereotypical (popular) categories.

Attali's phases mirror Baudrillard's mutation of the sign. Sacrificing is a diversion from the pain of the real and at the same time a reminder of class divisions. It is a counterfeit of someone else's enjoyment to help forget about one's own death, a kind of pacifier or production of class illusions. Representing is the means of reproducing the very idea of the value of capitalist markets in its products, production of production itself. Finally, repetition is the life blood of simulation. Consumers are most interested in collecting multitudinous signs of identity, a product of the consumption model.

Attali's application of Baudrillard's mutations of the self to the history of music inspired thesis and subsequent analysis of the relationship of the self to media culture.

The Direct Effects Paradigm of Mass Media Research and the Order of Counterfeit

The remainder of this chapter is a discussion of the discursive history of the first paradigm and the application of Baudrillard's idea of the counterfeit. The two come together in what I call the passive self. The study of the mass media goes hand in hand with the study of industrialized society and modernity. The three forces that created the age are industrialization, urbanization, and modernization. Industrialization was needed to support markets that were growing too large for the agrarian economy. Industrialization accomplished the production of more products, uniformity of product, advertising of products, and the creation of the need to consume products of industrialization. Urbanization also is more than just the result of young people moving into the cities to work and support the growing industrialization. Urbanization gave us a sense of living with one another as strangers yet working for an abstraction, a new age; the age is symbolized by modernity itself. Modernity is more than just industrialization and urbanization combined. Modernism is the full expression of the idea of progress and reproduction. All of these together created an undifferentiated aggregate known simply as the masses.

The model was already being used by social scientists in Europe when it first emerged as a model for American researchers in the 1930s (Beniger, 1987). Emile Durkheim (1933 in English), José Ortega y Gasset (1937), and the Frankfurt School (especially Adorno) all treated the emergence of a mass society and mass culture as a new phenomenon. Ferdinand Tönnies, Karl Mannheim (1935), and Max Weber would also come to have an effect across the Atlantic.

The mass media are assumed to have directly and symbiotically affected the development of the mass society. The mass media provided information about the spread of industrial knowledge and information about where development was occurring. It provided a sense of belonging to the masses, a closeness to one's neighbor even though the industrial worker was less likely than previous generations to know his neighbor. The mass media also provided a sense of political efficacy and expression, a modern scientific democracy. Therefore, to study the mass media was to study the mass society. The mass media act as a social barometer of the organizing and behavior of the nation.

The mass society theory, in its original form and its relationship with the mass media effects paradigm, lasted from the 1930s to the 1950s (Denliger, 1987). Many studies were accomplished under it. However, the initial paradigm is primarily defined by a body of research known as the Payne Fund studies, which supported strong uniform and lasting effects. Obviously, the body of work did not set out to define a field or even a paradigm. But it has become not only the benchmark, but a whipping post. By that I mean that the research has become known by what it lacked more than by what it contributed.

In this section, I want to show how the research created from the start a tension between levels of observation that would eventually destroy old paradigms and build new paradigms. I also want to show that although the two sides of the paradigm (i.e., magic bullet model and symbolic interactionism) created a sufficient tension for the field to be born and flourish, it is really false tension since theoretically the two sides of the model do not differ ontologically and they produce in the end the same product, a construction of the viewer.

A discussion of how the self is constructed in the paradigm will follow. I hope to show that the counterfeit self or the passive self is the result.

Magic Bullet Model

The magic bullet model rests on the assumption that a diverse mass society exists, but because diversity is Darwinistic under this view and individuals are influenced through their biology and emotions, diversity is narrow and easily assessed. If this is true then individuals can easily be seen as a unitary force, an audience, all with very similar bases of influence and interaction. The model here then for social researchers is a conservative, Watsonian behaviorism that assumes a uniform response across individuals. In other words, the model closely follows the transmission models spoken about earlier.

Shearon Lowery and Melvin DeFleur (1988) summarize the study of uniform influences of mass media messages in this way:

> 1) The media present messages to the members of the mass society who perceive them more or less uniformly,
> 2) Such messages are stimuli that influence the individual's emotions and sentiments strongly,
> 3) The stimuli lead individuals to respond in a somewhat uniform manner, creating changes in thought and action that are like those changes in other persons,
> 4) Because individuals are not held back by strong controls from others, such as shared customs and traditions, the effects of mass communication are powerful, uniform, and direct (pp. 21-22).

In the 1920s, there was great interest in the nature of films and their influence on an ever growing audience. The Payne Fund studies were funded by a philanthropic organization by the same name and welcomed by the motion picture industry.

Most of the research done during the Payne Fund studies took on the flavor of these assumptions. The general assumptions shaped the research questions and the methods used to advance the questions. The studies were primarily designed by scholars who concentrated on two broad areas: content and effects. More specifically, the researchers set out to assess the content of films, their ability to pass on information, change attitudes, stimulate emotions, harm health, and erode moral standards (Lowery and DeFleur, 1988).

The results support the general notions of the times that indeed film content dealt with the amoral or at least supported morals that did not match those of the population at large (Dale, 1935; Peters, 1933). In the context of the roaring twenties, it is easy to imagine that the creators of social policy went looking for problems. Remember that these boom times were met with abuses by the right in the establishment of Prohibition and the stock market. The results of the tests of influence of the mass media generally showed the same strength and direction of effects: strong and direct.

For example, the best known study within the Payne studies was the assessment of the effects of films on attitudes by Ruth Peterson and Louis Thurstone. The researchers tested six hundred adolescent subjects on their attitudes toward various racial and ethnic groups. They did this by establishing a pretest-posttest design. The treatment used was a film that was positively or negatively biased toward a racial or ethnic group. For example, *Birth of a Nation*, which is considered to portray African Americans in a negative light, and *Son of the Gods*, which is a positive treatment of Chinese, were used as treatments.

The experiment showed that there were statistically significant changes in attitudes toward the respective ethnicities after viewing a film. The studies also showed that the effects were cumulative in that if one viewing of a film did not influence an adolescent, two or three viewings would. Lastly, the researchers found that the effects persisted. This implies lasting attitude changes.

To a great extent, the findings were a product of the social theoretical assumptions outlined at the beginning of this section. The assumptions then influenced the methods used to assess film effects. Most of the research of the Payne Fund studies applied experimental or quasi-experimental methods. The methods limit the findings to direct strong effects or not and do not allow for varied reading of direct effects and limit the measurement of the strength of the effects.

The Payne Fund studies had an impact on communities inside and outside of the scholarly community. Outside of the academic community the findings were interpreted in a manner that was hostile to the film industry. A popular treatment by Henry Foreman (1933) was alarmist in tone. Many of the effects did not meet with the approval of parents and religious leaders. Interest in mass media effects at the general social level grew quickly as a result of the popular exposure had by the Payne Fund studies.

Most of all, the Payne Fund studies gave birth to organized, large-scale mass media effects studies. Later, the studies were rewritten into the history of the discipline. Its historical position is that it set a standard for all things to follow. This standard operates at many levels. First, it gave legitimacy to the scientific, empirical study of mass communication. In other words, it set in place a method to be used, tested, and verified. At another level, it puts in place a theoretical model to be reckoned with. The model fits a standard (or what would become a standard in rewritten history)—the previously mentioned transmission model that has been used to define and stabilize the field. These two level support the mass media effects school and strengthen and legitimize it.

At yet another level, the model is used by its critics. The mass media studies school uses the model to argue against the mass media effects position and to show the strengths of their own arguments. The argument that arises both weakens and strengthens their own orientation and the mass media effects school's orientation. First, it strengthens their side by arguing against a formal model. However, at the same time, although they present their own models, they must be put in the position of arguing against what is not their own. This inadvertently strengthens the mass media effects school. The mass media effects school gains "press" as it where. At the same time, the argument positions mass media effects as the dominant orientation. The argument also strengthens the mass media effects school by providing opposition to it. Formal opposition provides status for any incumbent source.

Overall, the argument that has arisen strengthens both schools of thought by causing them to evolve. The mass media effects school, as one might guess, has always come out ahead by virtue of its place in the argument, not necessarily because it is right.

Symbolic Interactionism

Symbolic interactionism is first and foremost a reaction to the loftier notions of human science, especially objectivity and prediction. Herbert Blumer (1969), who participated in the Payne Fund studies, said that symbolic interactionism is a more "down-to-earth approach to the scientific study of human life and human conduct" (p. 47). Furthermore, he wanted to include "subjective elements in sociological analysis of human society, yet the instruments (human documents) for getting such subjective elements do not allow us to meet the customary criteria for scientific data" (1979, xiii).

From its beginnings, symbolic interactionism and interpretive approaches in general were positioned as the opposition to dominant ways of thinking. This is especially true in the study of mass media use. The symbolic interactionists were outsiders to the idea of the passive viewer. They believed in a highly active and selective viewer. This, indeed, would become the prevailing attitude, but for the time being it was the minority view (Rogers, 1994).

However, the notion of an active viewer is problematic even today, primarily due to methodological problems. Interpretive theories take a much more subjective view, as the emphasis is placed on a way to explain the realm of individual consciousness, rather than mass appeal. Therefore, interpretive methods are usually less structured and more qualitative in nature. Interpretive research is more inductive, moving from the empirical to the theoretical. Theory is not used to drive hypotheses. Managing and interpreting the data is a primary concern with interpretive approaches. This is amplified by the fact that most interpretive data includes lengthy logs or diaries. The problem, however, is deemphasized by the richness of description that results (Rogers, 1994).

Interactionists believe in real, concrete, constructions of subjects. The subject acts toward things on the basis of the meaning that the things have for himself. The meaning of things arises out of social interaction. Lastly, subjects consciously modify meaning through an interpretive process which involves self-reflective individuals symbolically interacting with one another (Blumer, 1969).

Georg Simmel's theoretical perspective about communication is the starting point for symbolic interaction. Rogers (1994) summarizes Simmel's ideas this way:

1. Society, the core concept of sociology, consists of communication among individuals.
2. All human communication represents some kind of exchange that has reciprocal effects on the individuals involved.
3. Communication occurs among individuals who stand at varying degrees of social distance from each other.
4. Human communication satisfies certain basic needs, such as for companionship or aggression, or to pursue income, education, or other desired goals.
5. Certain types of communication become stable or fixed with time and thus represent culture and social structure (p. 150).

From there, Charles Cooley (1902) developed two main concepts. First was the idea of the primary group. The primary group is instrumental in the development of personality through socialization. Second, Cooley introduced the idea of the looking-glass self—the idea that human interaction reflects the immediate environment of the individual, thus serving as a mirror for the mind. Cooley's looking-glass self stresses the importance of interpersonal communication in personality socialization.

George Herbert Mead continued the development of symbolic interactionism with his definitions of the "self." In symbolic interactionism the self is a free agent but only within the boundaries set by the primary group or the society in general. Mead represented the self as the relationship between the "I" and the "me." Mead defined the "I" as the impulsive tendency of the individual's response to others. In contrast, the "me" is the incorporated others within the individual, consisting of all the attitudes of others with whom one has interacted and which one takes over into oneself. The "me" is thus an individual's view of how others see him or her—the attitudes of others that one assumes. An important concept for Mead was role-taking, the ability of the self individual to act socially toward himself or herself as toward others. Mead conceived of the mind as developing through communication with others.

Mead argued that no one is born with a self, and it does not develop instinctively. Instead, said Mead, "the self is developed through a social process of interaction with others" (Faris, 1970, p. 96). The individual internalizes the interpretations and meanings of various others, obtained particularly early in life, to create a "generalized other," which is built up from the averaged expectations of many other individuals. "The human, physiologically among the most helpless and dependent creatures in the animal kingdom, thus obtains an emergent power which makes him the dominant species on earth" (Faris, 1970, p. 98). The generalized other is those expectations of others with whom one interacts and who become a general guide to one's behavior. Gradually, an individual learns to act, not just in relation to the expectations of a few specific people, but in terms of how other individuals in general would expect one to behave. The essence of the self is reflexivity, the capacity to see oneself as an object of one's own reflection.

So how does the researcher study the individual and his necessary primary group? The subject is found out though his or her reports about the personal world. Therefore, symbolic interactionists posit language as the "window into the inner life of a person" (Denzin, 1992, p. 2). Furthermore, symbolic interactionists have generally been very interested in the relationship between man and communication technology. Early interactionists like Cooley were interested in the media's power to restore a sense of community. Each communication medium, over time, will to some extent determine the character of the knowledge communicated.

In the field of communication, Herbert Blumer is considered the first to apply symbolic interactionism to the study of mass media influences. The general purpose of his study as part of the Payne Fund studies was to assess how adolescents and young adults used movies in their play and daydreams. Over one thousand eight hundred participants wrote an autobiography of their personal experiences with and thoughts about movies. From the accounts, Blumer obtained general patterns of influence.

Blumer found in his analysis that movies had an influence on childhood play. Imitation of actors and situations dominated childhood play experiences. Imitation of roles also played a big part in social actions of children. The respondents remembered the mannerisms they picked up from the screen. Social learning about love and romance also happened in the opposite direction from screen to real life. Movies were also the source of fodder for daydreaming and fantasy. One of the most pronounced effects was deemed "emotional possession" (Lowery and DeFleur, 1988, p. 48). Blumer found that youths used certain movies for emotional stimulation or to manipulate their emotions.

Blumer had an influence on the field of mass media theory for years to come. His techniques and argument for face validity in analysis are still the source of debate. Probably the most important contribution made by Blumer's study is how it has been rewritten in history as the challenger to the dominant paradigm.

Blumer's study has been used as a benchmark for American cultural studies and the paradigm debates in mass media studies. In the tradition of George Herbert Mead, the leading philosopher in the the interactionist movement, Blumer followed an early cultural studies approach that examined the low culture, in this case movies, as something of a cultural phenomenon distinct from the cultural experiences with high culture. This distinction leads to two assumptions. The first has to do with class in that it is assumed that the primary users of low culture are those who participate in the popular culture. This class is, of course, the lower and working classes. This is not to say that the popular is not associated and consumed primarily by these classes, but further assumptions tend to stereotype the classes and their needs and lifestyles.

The other related assumption is that low culture is inherently vulgar. Vulgar here means more than just easily produced. Experiences with the vulgar as emotional appeal is emphasized. So, when Blumer went looking for effects, his methods may have been different but his assumptions would have been overwhelmingly biased. Norman Denzin (1992) writes that Mead and Blumer believed that moviegoers had inferiority complexes and were in need of daydreams and escape (p. 100). This elitist attitude went looking for the specific effects or, at least, the intensity of effects found.

Whether or not Blumer was a threat to the dominant perspective of the day is to be critically questioned. To be sure, Blumer's study was a qualitative study, as opposed to the quantitative studies that were the bulk of the Payne Fund studies. However, although the study is often posited as a more phenomenological approach than the other studies, it probably is not. As a matter of fact, the approach has been called behaviorist (Denzin, 1992, p. 3) and social psychological (p. 111). This labeling places this brand, at least, of symbolic interactionism in the same camp as the other studies in the Payne Fund and, more broadly, within the dominant paradigm, not outside or in opposition.

Denzin says of Blumer's theory:

> It presumed that the processes of identification, imitation, personification, and emotional possession produced a susceptibility to a film's effect. These effects were then realized directly in the form of imitation and personification and in their most extreme forms led to criminal conduct. The effects were then worked through the individual's existing scheme of life. In many cases they were stronger than influences of family, school, or church. The movies defined roles, impulses, emotions, and ideas for conduct (p. 111).

Blumer failed to recognize the role of family and neighborhood mediation of events, a cornerstone assumption of cultural studies today. It is assumed today that Blumer considered these prime determinants.

So, in review, the Blumer studies were forward looking in meaning-making (which reemerges later) but were not in their original form paradigm challenging. The studies were "trapped within a set of crippling assumptions concerning the movies and popular culture, the 'world out there,' social texts about the world, and the interpretive process and its relationship to an empirical science" (Denzin, 1992, p. 112).

However, in the rewriting of history, symbolic interactionism has been made to appear, more often than not as oppositional. First, the effects school uses it to point out its "non-empirical" nature and its comparative lack of control in method. This helps the mass media effects school to point to itself as the standard by which all things are measured. Media studies glorifies symbolic interactionism as at least a liberal starting point for interpretive social research. So, in the end, Blumer was trapped in the assumptions of his time but has been reconstructed as a founder of the field not because of his ideas but because of his assumed discursive position.

And so began a particular construction of the modern self that is the object of technology. In these early studies, the self is indeed a counterfeit and passive. The viewer is first and foremost a viewer. In both the Payne Fund studies and the symbolic interactionist approaches the individual merely takes on the attributes of the medium.

The medium also passes on values of its own. If the medium is corrupt then the viewer is corrupted. Or if the medium is fantasy then the individual is fantastic. Or if the medium transmits exaggerated class values then the individual begins to transcend class, yet at the same time begins to hate its ordinary class "skin." And so forth. The medium creates a prison house that is much more widespread and universal that ever before.

The movies and their passive viewers are counterfeits of one another. They stand concretely for one another due to the general assumption that individuals are the effect of the medium and vice versa. At the societal level, the aggregate effects are uniform and stand for an even better substitute for the content of the films. By this I mean that the consumer tries to be a better example than the one portrayed by films at least in public.

The consumer, under the illusion of the wealth of the movies, gains a social definition of their broad, common tastes—low culture. Being part of low taste culture not only positions one vis-a-vis those who appreciate high culture but also makes one aware of what is unachievable, thereby marginalizing one's tastes, despite the fact that they are in the majority. Therefore, movies in general as counterfeits remind us where we fit in and where we do not fit in the class/culture grid. Movies at this point are well known but mainly as kitsch. In the end, what is important here is that everyone knows the sign of the movies regardless of their "real" referent.

Chapter Four

The Active Self

The second paradigm, as said earlier, is either a refutation of the first or the first true paradigm that refutes the assumptions of an untested "first" paradigm. Those who argue the former know that the refutation aspect greatly strengthens and codifies their argument. It also strengthens the argument that the industrial world and the self have become completely modernized. The self has been to this point a post-Victorian passive subject and is now being readied for commodification by a complete reversal to an active, aware self, ready to take on the market. The active self is unencumbered by the media, full of choices, and unaffected. Herein lies the trap or illusion of freedom from media effects.

In theoretical terms, the interest was shifted from the individual as subject to the individual as object. In Baudrillard's terms, the self is now a sign in the production phase of the mutation of the sign. The self is introduced to its own importance in maintaining the advancement of capitalism.

The second order of signs refers to the boundless possibilities of mass production. The "energetic-economic myth proper to modernity" (1983b, 97) is the sign's Industrial Age purpose. Most signs that last come to convey the modern myth of production. The value of the industrial sign is no longer only in its referential value but in its commercial value vis-a-vis other signs and is "conceived from the point-of-view of [its] very reproducibility." (1983b, 100). To buy into the competition of signs and choosing a sign gives a stronger sense of belonging to industrial progress than holding a single counterfeit.

Media messages help us negotiate, not just the marketplace; they have become more important in the value of the product. What is popular is good; media are popular—media are good. This tautology makes the value inherent in the

49

individual product benign. Media are good, and more importantly, apolitical. As a result, they are not to be questioned.

At this point, to belong to the mass industrial society is increasingly important. The effect is much deeper in this phase. In some ways the active self believes he is the medium, not in the postmodern sense that we create the medium, but in the sense that individuals understand that they are the object of the market and must mediate messages sent to them. Media constantly remind individuals of their inclusion in the commercial environment. At the same time, media remind individuals of their own frail existence. Life expectancy of the very human, frail form is symbolically emphasized. The frailty of messages reminds the consumers of their own struggle to belong. Media help searchers find and channel themselves into increasingly marginalized, and lonelier, crowds.

Then that "map" becomes seemingly indistinguishable from the media business. The function of this reproductive sign is to define the benefits of mass production and marginalization to willing consumers. By reinforcing the myths of capitalism, especially its inclusiveness, the media sell the industry itself; the product becomes immaterial. The purpose of the second order sign is to promote the very idea of the industrial, scientific marketplace or capitalism. The grid becomes increasingly defined by the market and capitulation of the market.

The Second Paradigm: Limited Effects

Out of fear, social scientists tried to uncover the "secrets" behind moving the masses by the dictators of totalitarian states—Mussolini, Hitler, and Stalin. Of course, to teach and motivate our own populations was also of interest. Lasswell's model, mentioned in the second chapter, served well as a point of organization and departure. As research methods became more finely tuned and findings began to contradict uniform effects, a new, more sensitive model was built by Hovland and associates, who worked for the War Department and later would carry out hundreds of studies on mass media effects in the name of the Institute of Human Relations, which was funded by a Rockefeller grant to Yale University.

Learning theory was used to guide both theoretical inquiry and to organize teams of researchers. It is a simple linear model. It starts with basic behaviorist assumptions of stimuli, rewards, and reinforcement. The research question is: How does someone learn (become persuaded)? The model is simple with four parts: 1) attention; 2) comprehension; 3) yielding; 4) retention.

The logic of the model is that in order to persuade someone, we must first get their attention. Researchers studied just that. What are the best attention getters? And so the model continues. How are comprehension, yielding, and retention obtained?

Rogers (1994) writes:

> The independent variables are components in the Claude Shannon-type linear model of communication: SMCR (course, message, channel, receiver). Each of the Hovland-type experiments typically dealt with the effects of one dimension (or variable) of the SMCR components, for example, source credibility or fear

appeals, on attitude change. Such a single component approach rules out the study of interaction effects among the components as they act together to influence attitude change. Nevertheless, Hovland pursued the understanding of persuasion in such a concerted fashion over such a long period of years and with such considerable resources that the net result of his research program was a rather thorough understanding of attitude change behavior. Hovland was ingenious in designing one study to follow up on the leads from a previous experiment, with each investigation probing further into the behavior of study. In other words, Hovland carried out a research program in which the successive series of studies added up to a cumulative understanding of persuasion behavior that has never since been matched or even rivaled (p. 372).

More importantly, however, we can already see how the model differs from previous models. It is not a transmission-based model, but one that refers to the process of one person, the receiver. It has been called one of the first cognitive models.

However, we cannot be deceived so easily. In order to access any one of the four step, we must imagine the effects on one of those four steps. In doing so, we position the point of change in a receptor. In other words change is measured in a receiver. By the same token, antecedents are imagined in a sender, message, or channel. So, in essence there is no real change in the general assumption of the models. Learning theory is a transmission model in cognitivist clothing.

Learning theory did allow researchers to breakdown the effects process and examine the subtle differences in subjects or receivers. Upon finding differences in mass media effects depending on the receivers' characteristics (mainly demo and psychographics), the results were used to support what was to become known as limited effects paradigm.

The limited effects model is a response to the magic bullet model and times. The underlying assumptions and importance placed on emotions by the magic bullet were seen as wrong or at least not as powerful as a person's social background in predicting the outcomes of mass media influence. A person has various attitudes, values, beliefs, experiences, and needs that mediate messages. Therefore, a more active viewer is created. This is not the active viewer that we will come to know, one that very consciously chooses and interprets messages. This active viewer limits the power of mass media influence based on his or her own social limits, which influence the individual's "perceptual screens" (Lowery and DeFleur, 1988, p. 23).

The times also influenced this model of the individual. This model, which stressed social categories as the make-up of an individual, allowed the field of market research emerges. Social categories are a categorical language used to examine behaviors within and across groups. In addition to social categories, membership in social associations could also be mapped. Here the formal industrial grid of modernism is reified. Industry industrialized the audience in this way (this is where the Marxists that I'll talk about later come in).

The studies that first tested and best exemplify the notions of the limited effects model are the "Why We Fight Studies" done during World War II and Carl Hovland's continuation of those studies with the Yale Group following the war. The "Why We Fight Studies" assessed whether or not films had the power to improve factual knowledge, alter opinions and interpretations, change attitudes, and motivate actions (Lowery and DeFleur, 1988).

The findings were mixed. Acquisition of knowledge and effect on opinions were confirmed. Knowledge increased at an even greater rate depending on the education of the viewer. Opinion changes varied based on the nature of the presentation of the information. Film's influence on general attitudes were less profound. Motivation, the ultimate objective of the wartime studies, was not supported.

The importance of these results lies in their suggestion that effects depend on the characteristics of the message and the receiver. The Yale Group continued studying the effects of messages after the war. Most of the research helped researchers to refine techniques of message construction and build models of persuasiveness in individuals.

Overall, the limited effects model supported a direct effects paradigm that was mediated by techniques and social characteristics of the individual. In a way, the effects of the messages were not shown to be weaker. An argument can be made that forms of "noise," whether they are social characteristics or design differences, confounds or distorts the inherent effectiveness of the message. Therefore, effects are not weaker, they are just confounded.

Obviously, that would only speak to theoretical effects and not the very real ones found or not. There were limited effects to the respondents. Again, as in the magic bullet model, direction of effects could not be questioned because of the inherent limitations of the design. The next step to doubting the paradigm was already being determined in the research on the two-step flow.

Marxism/Technological Determinism

The active viewer begins to emerge with the rejection of the magic bullet model. The limited effects perspective rejected the notion that mass media users (note the term "users") determine their own use of a medium and can contend, using certain built in measures, to mediate effects. This is not to say (as will be later) that the control is conscious. Control, here, is akin to shaping and selection. In other words, different people consume differently. Symbolic interactionism was also attacked by structuralists (not linguistic structuralism, but social structuralism) as being too subjective and narrow in its perspective. Structuralists argue that individual behavior is shaped by economic and/or technological structures. All of this is not to say that the active viewer and its supporting theory replaced the magic bullet model. In the social sciences, in general, most "paradigms" are not replaced but are overshadowed or are subsumed into the newer view. Here, I will outline both economic and technological determinist schools of thought. I will start with Marx.

The Marxist point of view has been around since the beginning of communication studies in some form or another. Most would argue that the height of Marxian mass media studies occurred in the 1960s and '70s mainly with renewed interest in critical theory in Europe and newfound interest in it in America. Marxian interpretations of mass communication were really reactions to the dominant way of thinking and a complement to critical theory exploration. Traditional Marxist approaches were loosing steam in the 1960s and '70s because of newer and better interpretations of the political economy and because of general political biases in the United States. This section, then covers traditional Marxian scholarship before it mutated to critical theory. It includes, however, resultant neo-Marxian approaches, namely British cultural studies.

Marxists' vision of a viewer as the result of his or her place (class or culture or relationship to the mass media power centers) in society was affected by the mass media in some way. The "position" of a person is affected, which in turn places that person in a role. What affected the viewer is not the content of the messages, but the ideology of the institutions that controlled the airwaves. Marxists also focused on the ideology of advertising as a means of selling capitalism. But again, they cover advertising not as content but as a messenger of capitalism.

Others took a narrower, yet probably more totalizing view by focusing on television as a social narcotic—the new opiate of the masses. This view emphasizes television as a distraction from one's true position in society. We must remember that the two dominant metaphors here are drugs (in the Marxian view) and mind control (in the limited effects studies). America fought war with both in the mid-Cold War years. In the United States drugs were a seemingly unknown quantity. The fear was not so much of those using drugs but the possible spread of the usage and addiction. The Communist threat was as real. The Communists were not feared as much based on impending attack but from their mind control or subversive seductive ideology. The subversion extended to television.

> Marxists view capitalist society as being one of class domination; the mass media are seen as part of an ideological arena in which various class views are fought out, although within the context of the dominance of certain classes; ultimate control is increasingly concentrated in monopoly capital; mass media professionals, while enjoying the illusion of autonomy, are socialized into and internalize the norms of the dominant culture; the mass media taken as a whole, relay interpretive frameworks consonant with the interests of the dominant classes, and mass media audiences, while sometimes negotiating and contesting these frameworks , lack ready access to alternative meaning systems that would enable them to reject the definitions offered by the mass media in favor of consistently oppositional definitions (Gurevitch, 1982, p. 1).

Here, then, the two views of ideology and social narcotic are not contradictory but compatible. The small controversy posits the person differently in the acts of everyday life. The individual is both part of the dominant ideology and at the same time duped by the drug dealer that is television. This combining of macro and micro views benefits the totalizing perspective taken by Marxists.

So, the Marxist were armed and ready by the 1960s to say something about the mass media and its control. As they looked at the mass media varieties of

Marxism grew and flourished. The following is a review of the major points of view and their conclusions.

Classical Marxism is based on economism, which is the idea that economic conditions, as a "base," determine everything else in the superstructure (i.e. social, political, and intellectual realms of consciousness.) This basic type of Marxism is referred to as economic determinism or, later, vulgar Marxism. Marx had a specific type of economic determinism he called historical materialism. Under his view the mass media would be viewed as only a part of the means of production. In vulgar Marxism, the mass media is not seen as a product or producer of culture and its product is no different from any others. The mass media produces a product that is consumed by the masses. The product is sold by those who hold the means of production—the ruling class. So, for example, the ruling class sells a product (in most cases, sex and violence) that provides the largest possible profit.

The ruling class also sells the idea of the state and advertising support. In other words, the powers that be sell the very idea of capitalism. This in a simple sense is the selling of ideology. Classical Marxists speak about ideology, but subordinate it to the production process. This is a major objection to almost all other Marxian schools of thought. We will see that in other views, ideology takes a front seat to all other phenomena.

On the other hand, classical Marxists do believe that the mass media proscribe something outside the functions described above, and produce a "false consciousness." It works like this. The powerful product proscribed by the mass media is the values of the ruling class, which ignore diversity among the population and any argument for it. Marx said that the ruling class supplied the ideas to those who lack the means of mental production. So, in a more specific comment on duping, Marx did not necessarily believe that the masses were duped, but that they were already dupes ready for the taking—dupes with free choice. The mass media, in this case, would just act as a vehicle for expanding the economy of scale of the ruling class.

This would jive with Marx's intent. In his "materialist" philosophy, Marx believed that social being determined consciousness. Ideological positions are a function of class (remember that class distinction is determined by the political economy). Individuals come to know the media product from their class position. But they come to know their class positions as described by another about another (the ruling class position). This is done through the spread of false consciousness. False consciousness in the classical sense is the dominant values of the ruling class. By knowing these values the other classes are given something to emulate. This is the classical notion of the base affecting the superstructure.

In a more dialectical way of thinking, one might argue that the product is ruling class ideology, but instead of using it for purposes of emulation, one is reminded of his class and his place in society. Constant reminders weaken a sense of integration and strength. So, dialectically, the mass media and society reinforce the other. James Curran (1982) says, "ideology becomes the route through which struggle is obliterated rather than the site of struggle" (26).

Marxist interpretations of the viewer are many. One thing that is noticeable in the history of Marxist scholarship is that the viewer has been viewed as a passive more than he has active. Active viewing in a Marxist sense is the act of choosing merely to view or not. However, this choice too is determined through ideology or hegemonic forces. Therefore, the notion of viewing is still at the hands of a given ideology, dialectical relationship, structural category, cultural determinant, or hegemonic force.

Technological determinism holds that communication technology, rather than economics, determines history, social change, and social interaction. It is in this way then a theory that presume totalization. Technological determinism places communication in a dominant position of determining everything, giving it more reason for communication scholars to embrace it. This section first addresses technological determinism as a historical and social change theory. Then technological determinism as a social theory, in its many varieties, will be covered. Yet it is a step beyond a completely passive viewer in that it agrees with the limited effects model that posits the same structures as "allowing" for the viewer to be affected. The viewer mediates the mass media, not consciously, but with the structures of everyday life that flow through him or her.

Technological determinism has been a major force in the discipline of communication. Harold Innis and Marshall McLuhan both played key roles in calling the attention of scholars to the study of communication technologies and, more broadly, in popularizing communication study. To these two theorists, technology, or more precisely mass media technologies, are the sole antecedent causes of change in history and society. Technology is the fundamental condition underlying social organization. "Innis and McLuhan, alone among students of human society, make the history of the mass media central to the history of civilization at large. Both see the mass media not merely as technical appurtenances to society but as crucial determinants of the social fabric. For them, the history of the mass media is not just another avenue of historical research; rather it is another way of writing the history of Western civilization" (Carey, 1967).

In his first book, *The History of the Canadian Pacific Railway* (1923), Innis showed how construction of the railroad changed a society that had depended on waterborne transportation. Innis's "staples" maintained that the historical analysis of important raw materials, like furs and wood in the case of Canada, offers a means of understanding a nation's political economy. This line of thinking promotes a subtle materialism. However, in this case, the materials, not the economies of the materials, are the determinant to the political economy, not the other way round.

In *Empire and Communications* (1950) and *The Bias of Communication* (1951), Innis viewed communication mass media as the very essence of civilization. He "pursued communication in a genuinely interdisciplinary way. He . . . restored communication study to an historical foundation" (Carey, 1981). In *Empire and Communication*, Innis contended that communication media are "biased" in terms of their tendency to permit control over time or space. The mass media used in ancient civilizations, like clay, parchment, and stone, were durable but difficult to transport. These time-biased mass media are conducive to control over time but not over space. On the other hand, papyrus and paper are space-biased. Space-biased mass media promote geographical extension of empires and encouraged military expansion.

The time/space dichotomy can be used to look at the growth of civilization or to describe a given society. For example, space-biased societies are characterized by stable and hierarchical social orders, which stifle individualism as a potential agent of change. Time-biased communication systems are found in societies with a rich oral tradition or with written technologies where access is limited to a privileged few. Therefore, by knowing the dominant communication technology of a time we can know its mode of control and the likelihood associated with it.

Space-biased communication media are oriented to the present day and to the future. The emphasis is on expansion, an increase in political authority, and creation of secular institutions, with the subsequent growth of science and technical knowledge. Societies with space-biased communication media are characterized by highly efficient systems of information exchange and mass communication. Although these systems are functional, they cannot convey the richness of the oral tradition. Print, telephone, radio, and television are space-biased.

McLuhan claimed that when print media began to replace certain oral communication, the seeing/hearing sensory ratio was changed, leading to changes in how individuals perceive information and thus in how they think. The introduction of the phonetic alphabet, for example, led to linear thinking as individuals followed left-to-right sentences. McLuhan saw communication technology as a main cause of social change, especially at the individual level.

So then, technology determines history along two lines. First, we have seen that technologies define the era and epochs of linear history. Second, technological determinism can be used to describe a given time and used to determine the social conditions and movements of the given time. Within a given epoch then, how can we predict the impact of a medium or media and determine its dominance? This is the next question we must ask of technological determinism as a deterministic theory.

To answer this question we must determine whether or not technological determinism is a reductionist or holistic theory. Technological determinists debate this in several ways. Reductionists argue that technology causes effects in all other known forms, i.e., the individual, historical, and the social. This scientific explanation is monocausal in its approach. One must assume that there is a dominant technology and determine it a priori. Holists believe that media technology are part of a social grid that strongly determines how we interact at the social and interpersonal levels. This technological grid defines the common sense relationships of everyday life.

This debate reminds us of the strong economic determinism versus a more dialectical materialism in the Marxian interpretations. Does the technology alone shape outcomes or does technology form a structure from which outcomes are shaped?

To argue this relationship between technology and social outcomes, theorists go back to the determinist theory of linguistic relativity. (Stuart Hall and

John Fiske do the same thing in developing a new Marxism and fortifying their own theories.) Linguistic relativity (or sometimes called the Whorfian hypothesis) argues that our actions and culture are determined by our language (the problem of that even in this theory there is argument over whether the language itself determines outcomes or determines a structure from which outcome fit). Technological determinists assume that as toolmakers our most basic of tools is language; thus we can begin to argue that communication technologies are just extensions of our human language. McLuhan equated technologies with language. However, he vacillated on the question at hand as to whether technologies influence us directly or if they set a grid. It seems that when it came to talking about individuals, he stressed the former strong relationship between technology and humans. When he spoke of history, he used the latter explanation. In any case this debate has caused sides to be drawn between "hard" technological determinists and "soft" determinists. The "hard" technological determinists believe that technology determines or at least is necessary for change (see Finnegan). In their view, media are autonomous, apart from our social relationships and grids but very influential on them. At the individual level, each technology has its own characteristics which determine our uses of it and our relationship with it. "Weak" determinists see technology as facilitating a grid or at least creating the potential for opportunities of change (see de Sola Pool). They also see the choice to use technology as important.

The process of reification is often debated and used by weak technological determinists to illustrate our relationship with technologies. Reification is the process by which we, as individuals, make something abstract concrete. This can happen in many directions. A computer can be reduced to a word processor, or it can be likened to another more familiar object, like the typewriter. The process further reduces the new technology to a thing among things. The computer becomes a machine among a field of machines. At one level then we can see that we may, through reification, make a machine autonomous. But more than likely, reification is a process that makes us commit to a symbolic world to which we are manifest.

One of the most famous theorists along these lines is Jacques Ellul. He argued that technologies are attributed to a world of technique, which represent a place of methodological rationality and absolute efficiency. Each new technology adds to the mix and, at the same time, the newer technologies (computers and television) blur the distinctions between technologies and between us and technologies. This creates an environment of subservience (and love) to technique. Ellul said, "Technique has become autonomous; it has fashioned an omnivorous world which obeys its own laws and which has renounced all tradition" (Ellul, 1964, 14). This suggests a shift from intellectual processing and thinking to mere practice and work. It also suggest that technology now begets technology and that the world of technological autonomy is a natural or at least has become a natural occurrence and force. Therefore, Ellul might say that we have created an autonomous code for technology. A code here is something that shapes our assumptions about the world and works like a language. In the end technology's effects are inevitable and unpredictable.

Do any theorists believe that we predict technological effects? The technological imperative view is autonomous but that we ought to take advantage of it before it takes advantage of us. In other words, we must get ahead of the "technological curve" to understand it and to create our own destinies (see Pacey, 1983). Individuals have a choice in their adoption of technologies but must realize that in any event they will be controlled by the use of technologies. The result of such thinking is to treat people not just as the byproducts of technology but as technologies themselves. Technological imperative type of thinking "technologizes" people, forcing them to act as machines in the regulation of machines. To follow the imperative then is to have no choice but to follow the choice of mechanization. The belief is that by forming a special relationship with technologies we will come to formulate all technological problems using our own technological solutions.

A less extreme view is held by Neil Postman, who believes that technologies are autonomous, yet non-neutral. He denies that "'the effects of technology are always inevitable' yet, 'always unpredictable'"(1983, 24). Therefore, he sees the world as a place in which humans deal with media that are critically deconstructable and understood and controllable but that there are always unforeseen and unknown results. Postman (1979) uses a critical approach to describe why the media are non neutral and there unpredictable. He argues:

(1) because of the symbolic forms in which information is encoded, different media have different intellectual and emotional biases;
(2) because of the accessibility and speed of their information, different media have different political biases;
(3) because of their physical form, different media have different sensory biases;
(4) because of the conditions in which we attend to them, different media have different social biases;
(5) because of their technical and economic structure, different media have different content biases (1979, 193).

So, Postman argues not that technology itself is not to be understood but that the frames of interpretation are always precarious in respect to the seemingly neutral idea of technology. These frames are intellectual, emotional, political, sensory, social, and content. Technologies are simply metaphors through which we conceptualize reality. They are not merely information conduits between the technological and social world.

In summary, weak technological determinists are divided on the mechanics of the effects, but more importantly, the basic notion of technological effects and their predictability. Ellul believes that we interact with technology to reify it the level of discourse that has become our greatest social control, therefore losing sight of its effects and, therefore, its predictability. Imparativists see technology as being predictable through control of its development and knowledge of choice. However, in the end, they believe that this is too difficult a challenge. Neil Postman argues a neo-McLuhanist view that says we could foresee the effects of technology if we could hold the frames (contexts) in place. But with the frames of life becoming even more relative and subjective, prediction becomes very difficult. Postman has often said that he himself does not know about what technology does, he only knows what it has undone. This illustrates a position that emphasizes our blind use of technology and its effects on the very frames that we should be using to judge the effects of technology. It also brings us full circle to McLuhan, who believed that current technology cannot be evaluated on its own terms; it can only be understood in terms of that which preceded it in terms of the dominant technology and social impact.

There are two other "technological as neutral" views, but they are not really technological determinist in their orientation (although they may be a reaction to technological determinism). One can guess that one is the technologies are neutral school of thought. This non-theoretical stance discredits any technological determinist stance as wrong. Technologies have no impact outside of our own use of them. Technologies are our inventions and clearly under our control. Tools are not extensions of our human nature, just something we do. "Technology is not neutral" is another stance that looks at the direct impact of technology on society. This is not however, a pure technological determinist stance because these theorists attribute the reasons for technologies not being neutral to their political, economic, social, or critical manipulation. Therefore, the emphasis in this stance is on an antecedent that might be used in a Marxian, cultural, or critical theory, covered elsewhere in this chapter.

In the end, views of our relationship with technology vary in intensity and mechanism, but all hope for a truly self-aware individual who understands the limits of his choice. Alas, almost all of the theorists above agree that individuals are too closely intertwined with the media to the point that they can't escape. Individuals believe that a strong relationship with the dominant medium gives them greater choice and free will.

In this way, the theories addressed in this chapter point to a self that believes that media provide a path to the modern industrial age, in which the self has an active will to make choices from an endless array of choices. Naming one's choice, however, is a trap that leads to defining one's self on the social grid. The grid really names the choices and they are universal. In this way the map (grid) then becomes what is real. The self is mainly a confluence of points on the grid. The self is now ready for packaging.

Chapter Five

The Commodified Self

The third paradigm constructs a commodified self who is more than just a consumer. The self in this case is the common consumer—the mirror image or simulation of the market. In this chapter, Baudrillard's arguments toward a commodified self is covered, followed by a discussion on how this theoretical self is supported by the third paradigm.

Beyond Commodification

Jean Baudrillard was born in Reims in 1929—as he points out, the year of the first great crisis of modernity, the Great Depression. Early in his career, Baudrillard was influenced by Henri Lefebvre's *Critique of Everyday Life* (1958). Lefebvre argued that everyday life has ceased to be a "subject" rich in subjectivity: it has become an "object" of social organization. He meant that individuals have less control in self-realization (subject) and adopt market categories to describe themselves (object). Individuals objectify the self and themselves. The self has become, through market categories, an object of market dimensions and dynamics. This is a simple psychodynamic method of explaining the commodification of the consumer. More important, it sets in place a mechanism that defines the individual from the outside, rather than from the inside.

As a structural Marxist, Baudrillard easily embraced these ideas. Lefebvre's critique contained some of the traditional and newer Marxist ideals. The traditional Marxist argument of commodification and object fetishism is followed closely. The critique still stressed a Marxian orientation to the worker's point of view and the concept of alienation, but Lefebvre theorized that the mode of production had stalled. Many of his contemporaries agreed. Production no longer determined consumption or the resultant social structure (Baudrillard, 1968).

In order to increase production and support for an ever-growing and richer elite, it was essential that consumption become the basis of social order. Buying into a category of the market increased consumption, yet also began to define the nature of the individual. In other words, if a consumer wanted to "fit in," he or she had to buy the representations of that category. At the same time, the category defined not only the priorities of the individual, but also the idea of what an individual of that ilk does and is. The inclusion of a psychodynamic dimension begins to become a point of analysis. Baudrillard agreed with this idea but would quickly go at least one step further.

In the 1960s, Paris was the site of riots by groups who called themselves the enrages, a group associated with the Situationists International. The Situationists, most of whom were students, believed that modern society had lost its spontaneity and had become passive. Consumption had become the opiate of sorts (drug and dealer in one). They invoked the language of the structural linguists, reducing modern society to mere consumers of the sign—the overarching sign of consumerism. The inferences of the Situationists were two: that language is at the center of the method of analysis and that belief pointed to language as the consumption of messages. This connoted an adoption of a general belief system, one that revolved around commodification. The sign is consumed and is consuming.

Baudrillard considered the ideas of the Situationists, but only for a short time. After a while, he decided that they were wrong. He believed that capitalism does not repress participation but encourages it. The problem is that we participate with signs and networks of signs and not with each other. Our interactions with one another are suppressed and displaced.

This is where Baudrillard breaks from Lefebvre and the Situationists. Participation in the consumer society, then, is active. Baudrillard believed that consumption is not a "passive process of absorption and appropriation" (1982, p. 199), as it was in the age of the mode of production. "Consumption is an active form of relationship, a mode of systematic activity and global response which founds our entire cultural system" (p. 199).

Baudrillard was not alone. Guy Debord's *Society of the Spectacle* (1967) led Baudrillard to reexamine the ideas of the Situationists. Debord's landmark book is important at one level in that it was an attempt to explain the amorphous notion of the new, more powerful sign. Although not directly defined in the book, the sign is illustrated by example or implication. The book is also important for its style. The use of "posting theses" that build and reiterate ideas also represents the notion of fragmentation of the self, often discussed in the postmodern literature. This starts a "tradition" (attempted in this work as well) of writing in oscillating styles to illustrate the nature of the work.

The sign is described in a few select theses. In the first, Debord states that individual and society are an "accumulation of spectacles . . . all that once was directly lived has become mere representation" (p. 12). Debord's dialectic is one in which the image opposes reality in devising a new ideal, the spectacle. This most certainly influenced Baudrillard. For Baudrillard, the created thing is the only thing, the hyperreal—the expected, not the mundane. The spectacle is the new false consciousness, a false consciousness not emitted by the worker, but by a consumer apprehended by the sign.

By the fourth thesis, Debord reveals the postmodern sign. "The spectacle is not a collection of images; rather, it is a social relationship between people that is mediated by images" (p. 12). The sign is the adoption of images for the purpose of constructing the self and social discourse. These images are not attached to anything and no one has any responsibility for them. Debord claims that signs are a common stream of deceit and differences. This was a bold statement. However, it has become the most influential theme of poststucturalists. The poststructural sign is discourse and the discourse defines difference, not similarities to a model or ideal. If we believe in the sign for itself exterior of ourselves, then it is true that the sign serves a dividing, delineating function or a "differend." In short, it is a lie.

In the fifth thesis, Debord makes clear that the spectacle is just another materialist reality. He says that the sign is a "world view transformed into an objective force" (p. 13). With all the strength of Hegel, Debord sees the imaginary construction of a force that turns back on its creator to control him or her. This construct is then used to objectify the self, apart from any notion of personal choice or identity.

Baudrillard wrote about this later in *The System of Objects* (1968). Participation with objects makes us think of the functions of the things in our lives. In doing so, we reduce ourselves to functional beings. We make ourselves functional to the things most important in our age, e.g., commercialism and technology. We are stripped of symbolism and expression. We act only as a cybernetic consumer, responding to a market of signs.

Choice is the ideology of consumption. Choice is imposed on us. This is true of any element of ideology. The difference today is that choice is not a powerful tool outside ideology, used to choose a belief system. Nor is choice a tool used within the ideological system used to develop a belief system. Choice is the dominant ideology. Although an awkward way of expressing it, choice is already chosen in the system. In previous days, consumption contained choice. Choice was used to differentiate selected options. Now, the new logic of choice contains the rules of consumption. The new choice is singular—to belong or not.

And if consumption is related to fetish, it is related in reverse today. No longer is fetish produced from consumption. In many ways, all that is left is fetish, fetish of consumption. We no longer choose what to fetish. Fetish itself is to belong to the postmodern consumer society. New choice defines new freedoms (or lack thereof) and the individual (or lack thereof). We are shaped by the choices given to us, the greatest of which is the illusion of choice. Baudrillard believes:

> No object is proposed to the consumer as a single variety. We may not be granted the material means to buy it, but what our industrial society always offers us a priori as a kind of collective grace and as the mark of formal freedom, is choice. This availability of the object is the foundation of "personalization":

only if the buyer is offered a whole range of choices can he transcend the strict necessity of his purchase and commit himself personally to something beyond it. Indeed, we no longer even have the option of not choosing, of buying an object on the sole grounds of its utility, for no object these days is offered for sale on a "zero-level" basis. Our freedom to choose causes us to participate in a cultural system willy-nilly. It follows that the choice in question is a specious one: to experience it as freedom is simply to be less sensible of the fact that it is imposed upon us as such, and that through it society as a whole is likewise imposed on us. Choosing . . . may personalize a choice, but the most important thing about the fact of choosing is that it assigns you a place in the overall economic order (1968, p. 141).

In *The System of Objects* (1968), Baudrillard explores the possibility that consumption has become the chief basis of the social order. Consumer objects constitute a classification system and have their effect in structuring behavior. The object has its effect when it is consumed by transferring its "meaning" to the individual consumer. A potentially infinite play of signs is thus instituted that orders society while providing the individual with an illusory sense of freedom (Sarup, 1992, p. 161).

Mass production has given us uncountable products. The similarity of the functionality of the products should discourage the level of consumerism currently experienced. To be mass consumed, the series must be customizable, they must have the ability to "accessorize." The sign enables us to seemingly personalize objects.

Baudrillard builds on Daniel Riesman's (1953) idea that inessential differences are what creates demand. Demand then responds to personalization of the object. This "secondary seriality constitutes fashion" (Baudrillard, 1968, p. 142). Distinction or difference then constitutes the object from which it was modeled (the "original") and then erases the model. The model becomes only an idea. Although contained in each of the series, the model is not bound itself to any history or class. As a matter of fact, the model as idea releases itself from history while, at the same time, embodying all of its developmental history.

Upon erasing its model and history, the serial is free to float and point to a cultural system of personalized consumption.

The fact that the model is just an idea is the thing that makes personalization possible. The notion that consciousness could be personalized in an object is absurd: it is personalized rather, in a difference, because only a difference, by referring to the absolute singularity of the model, can thereby refer at the same time to what is really being signified here, namely the absolute singularity of the user . . . Paradoxically, then, it is through an idea that is both vague and shared by all that everyone may come to experience himself as unique . . . [S]elf-individuality on the basis of the range of serial distinctions that allows the imaginary consensus of the idea of the model to be revived. Personalization and distinction go hand in hand. That is the Miracle of the system (Baudrillard, p. 144).

In *Consumer Society* (1970), Baudrillard looks at systems of signs that differentiate the population. "Difference—in this case cultural difference—is what creates value, and it has to be paid for" (p. 151). "This is the ideological function of the system: increasing status is nothing but a game, for all difference is integrated in advance. Consumer objects are best understood not as a response to a specific need or problem but as a network of floating signifiers that are inexhaustible in their ability to incite desire" (Sarup, p. 162).

The Third Paradigm

The two-step flow and uses and gratifications are usually seen as a phase of the limited effects paradigm. However, I have given them special consideration because of their unique explanations of media effects, bridge to the next level of the paradigm, and, mostly, because of the general positive disruption both gave to the tradition of the mass society theory.

Moderate Effects

Two-Step Flow: The People's Choice

Starting in the 1950s with research done on voting behavior and continuing through contemporary diffusion of innovation research, researchers began to discover that the effects of the media were somewhat stronger than expected especially within the context of the social group or network. Effects are heightened based on direct contact with information sources, which can be media and/or individuals who act as our media filters and authorities, otherwise known as opinion leaders. Social groups—friends, family, acquaintances, etc.—come to bear on decisions regarding behavior toward the mass media. Patterns of attention to the media are also shaped by social ties and networks (Lowery and De-Fleur, 1988). Therefore, media have selective and indirect influence that may be stronger in its overall influence than previously suspected. This perspective, then, is a shift in the paradigm in that it discounted direct effects assumptions.

Elihu Katz and Paul Lazarsfeld (1955) are responsible for the research on what became known as the "two-step flow of communication." We will turn to that research in a moment. However, the initial notions of a two-step flow of communication begin with studies on voting behavior (Lazarsfeld, Berelson, and Gaudet, 1948).

In May of 1940, a group of researchers from Columbia University began to research of voting behavior in Erie County, Ohio. The work that they began there became known as "The People's Choice" project. The purpose was to uncover how people made their decision during an election period.

The researchers sampled some three thousand respondents. One group of six-hundred was followed for six months prior to the election and the month following the election that pitted Roosevelt against Dewey. Three control groups were used, each with six hundred respondents at crucial times during the period. One group was surveyed after the Democratic convention, another following the

Republican convention. The third control group was surveyed right before the election.

Besides uncovering voters' predispositions to one or the other party and assessing voters' knowledge and interest, the group determined that the media had a role in voter decisionmaking. They found that the media influence voters in three ways: activation, reinforcement, and conversion. Activation is the process of activating latent predispositions. About 14 percent of voters are aroused by propaganda that increases interest levels. Then the voter relies on latent predisposition to selectively attend to and retain messages. The latent then becomes manifest in what the researchers called vote crystallization.

About 50 percent of voters use the media to reinforce their vote. Media give the users ammunition for debate and reason to participate. When the media can't do that conversion may occur among 8 percent of voters and if it does happen will occur earlier rather than later.

The "Peoples Choice" research made two unexpected theoretical statements. First, the research seriously weakened the assumptions of the magic bullet. Voters were highly selective based on the interest. They were not all the same and were more proactive than previously assumed. Second, upon reviewing their observations, they knew that they had not put enough stock in the conversations that people had about politics. They hypothesized that most people got their information from others who in turn got their information from many places including the media. They set off to test this hypothesis in what would come to be known as the two-step flow hypothesis.

Two-Step Flow: Personal Influence

Testing the two-step flow hypothesis relies on the assumption that individuals reside in various "primary groups," (Rothlisberger and Dixon, 1939) within which they create meaning. Two-step flow asks: From where does their information come? The answer is, from "opinion leaders." The researchers proceeded to study how opinion leaders could be identified.

Lazersfeld and Katz clearly found that opinion leaders influenced others and that their means of information were usually the media. The research is important in various ways. First, it laid to rest the magic bullet. Clearly individuals were not strongly influenced by the media, nor were they directly influenced all the same way.

The research is also important in that it shifted influence based solely on individual characteristics to social, small group characteristics. This is important in two ways. First, it broadened the scope of the study of media effects. This is certainly the effect of good thinking, but the influence of earlier thought (i.e., symbolic interactionism and Marxism) can't go unnoticed. Even more important to the present study is the notion of an internalized group or general self-awareness attributed to the self. Unlike symbolic interactionism, the self is not a psychically formed or formulated group but a real, internalized group, one that includes the notion of belonging and all the things that come with belonging, e.g., acceptance, rejection, embarrassment, competition, loss, and discovery. The project would be continued for many years.

Everett Rogers's *Diffusion of Innovations* (1962) developed a model of media influence within his greater model, which dealt with appropriate channels for the successful adoption of an idea, practice, or object. Of course, media are some of many channels, but it is an important one depending on the culture, who the innovators and early adopters are, and where the innovation is in the adoption process. The process includes four phases: knowledge, persuasion, decision, and confirmation.

In this way, the diffusion model emphasizes situations. Influence, whether it is mediated or not, depends on the context. Just as the process must change with a situation, so is the self considered changing based on contextual forces. In addition, the work extended the findings of the two-step flow by emphasizing social forces, but by also showing that many different groups exist not based on interest but by the contextual strengths of their interaction. Social cognition was at its height in the understanding of social processes and the media.

The search for primary groups and opinion leaders is heavily used in marketing even today. Marketing models of the times went hand in hand with the above communication models. Both market research techniques and communication research were coming of age together. During that time, a new individual was created. The individual was characterized by where they stood in the marketing chain based on the variables that they themselves characterized, manipulated, emphasized, or suppressed. The self was one that became very aware of itself as consumer in the overall model and was also quite conscious of its delivery to the market, not as an individual affected as everyone else by the market, but one that was different yet bundled and delivered to the market with like selves.

To the self this is a more liberated model than the one that sees the self as the same as as everyone else and affected equally by the media. However, the illusion of choice is just that. The self sees itself as part of various groups and being accepted. This is much more humane than the previous models. But at the same time, those groups are mostly defined by what they consume, their likelihood to consume, and ability to consume, whether it's news, soap, or gossip. The self chooses characteristics that are defined by the group, which has been defined by the market. The self is under the illusion of choosing the characteristics. Therefore the self is one of the consumers.

The self is also part of a network of consumers who vary by interests. As interests change so do the networks. The market in this case doesn't like such change as it will in the future, because of the rise of the audience—the thing to which everyone will desire to belong. The self goes beyond demographic description to sociographic or taste distinctions.

Uses and Gratifications

The uses and gratifications approach assumes that individual differences among mass media users cause them to seek out messages that gratify some need. Rather than focus on external effects, the uses and gratifications approach examines motivations and behaviors. Therefore, the approach assumes that the audience is active. Some users are more active than others but their behaviors are purposive and goal seeking. These goals may be either part of rituals or be more instrumental (Rubin, 1984).

The approach stems from functional psychology in which psychological needs are consciously assessed and gratified. Early researchers identified media functions. Lasswell (1948) identified three major functions of the mass media. First, he wrote that the media keep viewers aware of their environment. This is the "eyes and the ears" of the public, as it has become known. Second, the media serve a correlation of environmental parts. This is to say that the media provide information with which users can develop opinions. Third, the media transmit social and cultural norms to new viewers. Others added more functions of the media to the list. Charles Wright (1960) added entertainment. Donald Horton and Richard Wohl (1956) added parasocial relationship, the personal relationship that is felt by the user with characters or other mass media figures, to the list. Others—escapism (Pearlin, 1959), anxiety reduction (Mendelsohn, 1963), and play (Stephenson, 1967)—have also been added.

By the 1970s, researchers began to ask users themselves how media functioned in their lives. Not only were these researchers following up on the earlier tradition, they wanted to develop a viewer who was rational and in conscious control of his or her choices. So, although they used similar methodologies to those of their media effects colleagues, their concept of the user was much more liberal and self-conscious.

Elihu Katz, Michael Gurevitch, and Hadassah Haas (1973) performed the first large-scale research using the approach. They found that the mass media are used to gratify many needs, both psychological and sociological, such as self-understanding, relationship development, and social transmission. Following Katz et al., a large group of scholars proceeded to develop typologies of viewers, which caused very little controversy and the literature is too large to go into here. Suffice it to say that the approach spawned an industry.

Most importantly, uses and gratifications scholars developed a methodology, largely using survey techniques, and a motive. However, they lacked a comprehensive theory. So, they set off to find one. This quest is where we find a more accurate view of the self in their research.

Jennings Bryant and Susan Thompson (2002) identify four models used to explain uses and gratifications. The first is the transactional model (McLeod and Becker, 1974), which combines the direct effects model with the individual differences model. Simply, effects depend on an individual's involvement with the message. The second was the gratification seeking and audience activity model (Rubin and Perse, 1987), which adds the level of viewer's attention and previous attitudes to involvement. Third, expectancy value (Palmgreen and Rayburn,

1982) predicts effects based on the viewer's expectancy and evaluation. Expectancy is the perceived consequences of holding or changing an attitude or of a behavior. Evaluation is the degree of effect. Lastly, the uses and dependency model (Rubin and Windahl, 1986) focuses on dependency on particular technology, which in turn limits the viewpoints or alternatives.

As one can easily see, the first three theories or models that were meant to explain uses and gratifications gravitate to a strong media effects position. As a matter of fact most research done in this tradition today is referred to as uses and effects. The uses and dependency model attempts to define social conditions available to an individual or competitive forces among media. This remains somewhat in the mass media studies tradition.

So, why include uses and gratifications in the media studies tradition? Simply put, the uses and gratifications model was used to argue against mass media effects models that proponents thought were too behavioral in their approach. Looking back, however, we can see that uses and gratification was at its center a behavioral model only of the functional type, which is even more simplistic than the operant types of models of the day.

More theoretically however, although the model became more like the effects models and uses a more quantitative approach to assessment, uses and gratifications is a mass media studies model due to its initial strong position of a rational self with free will, choice, and who is self-conscious. Also, in the functionalist tradition, an attempt was made to speak to social norms and conditions. The problem was, however, the uses and gratifications model was "too individualistic" (Bryant and Thompson, 2002, 133) and difficult to extend to society.

"Too individualistic and difficult to extend to society." This sounds like a criticism of Soviet Communism. Uses and gratifications was in the same situation as Soviet Communism in that it proported to be a liberal alternative but underneath it was incredibly conservative and self-consuming. In the case of uses and gratifications, the individual is made quite aware of its role in consumption of capital goods. The consumer is at the heart of uses and gratifications, which is the modeled after marketing type research, the focus group extrodinaire. It constructs a consumer who gets what he or she wants.

The model may have failed, but it was influential in defining a liberated self that defined itself rather than being defined by external forces or determined by internal limitations. This lasted a short while. However, no matter how the user was defined, he was still a user. Users, just like addicts, are never in control. Although they may have more control than the passive viewer, they are still described in terms of the technology and markets. The user is functionalized. In that, I mean that the user is made up of functions that are made up of needs to which the market is correlated. Wanting to know those functions is only wanting to know how to deliver bundles of individuals to the market.

What is most interesting about the two-step flow and uses and gratifications is their orientation to the market and market research. The two models come together with the previous models to cover all areas of the market. The second paradigm focused on demographics. The models discussed in this chapter add sociographics, taste cultures, and psychographics to the mix. In this way a market is completely analyzed and packaged as an audience. Selves were analyzed as they truly were becoming—the marketplace. Individuals mirror the market to the point of simulating the market. They are more than consumers, more than commodified—they are becoming hypercommodified.

This is not to say, at least not at this early juncture, that the self is not active. It is active in a different way than before. Previously, the active self had complete choice. Here the self believes that in order to have greater choice it must limit choices in order to make itself more efficiently deliverable to the market.

Simulation goes beyond industrialization. Individuals construct all meaning and seemingly the market. "I get what I want" becomes the consumer's mantra. The market merely provides signs the consumer has asked for to gratify emotional needs. Choice is the dominant ideology and allows individuals to accessorize to meet the expectations of the audience to which they belong. But as in all of the levels of the sign, contradiction maintains stability. In this case we get an audience that believes that "audience" is synonymous with "society." The need to fit into audiences created by the mass media erases the social. This will be crystallized over the following thirty years.

Chapter Six

A Turn to the Teleself

In the last two chapters we have seen the self readied for packaging and then packaged as a marketable item. We have exhausted Baudrillard's original model, covering mutations from counterfeit to production to simulation. Now, the self is ready to become a model that really doesn't exist outside market researchers' and academics' minds. This simulacrum is known as the audience. People become different when they are part of an audience. They have different expectations, believe they are more powerful and have more control than they really do, and construct themselves differently in that they turn the tables and package themselves to be marketed.

The current paradigm, a fermentation of the proceeding steps, reinforces this notion. The new paradigm is one that has revived or is reviving the strong effects orientation but this time is "made up of atomized individuals at the mercy of centralized media" (Beniger, 1987, p. 51). Individuals exhibit control based on their general understanding of the mass media system, what it offers, and an understanding of the information at hand (cognitive map). Schema are adopted, not constructed, and fleshed out over time. Or, as Doris Graber (1984) wrote, "Mass media messages are not imprinted on the minds of mass media audiences in the precise manner in which they are offered. Rather, audience members condense the offerings in their own ways, select aspects of interest, and integrate them into their own thinking" (p. 209).

The problem is that no one can comprehend the media system. Its explosion presents a moving target that is not only speedy but constantly fragmenting and at the same time consolidating. The model that is drawn comes from the dominant media. The self constructs itself as a higher level simulacrum by adopting the model and using that same model to censor information. This eventually results in the construction of nonsense at the linguistic level, which the new tele-self uses to construct himself.

The Social Grid as Audience Grid

In an advanced capitalist society, the social grid is defined most closely and directly though the audience grid. Categories that formulate the empirical audiences come from many places. The audience is so immersed in the environment of the marketplace that the categories that the audience ascribes to go unnoticed. However the audience is portrayed by the market as a commodity, numbers, individuals, or spectators (Blumler, 1996). The viewer as commodity reduces the watching of television to a transaction. In order to know whether to buy into something he or she sees, the viewer must label him or herself a possible buyer. The possibility of buying is defined by the categorical match between the buyer and seller. Therefore, in the process the buyer must label him or herself more precisely using the demographic characteristics of market research.

Michel Foucault (1982) and Ian Hocking (1981, 1982) come to similar conclusions about the nature of the individual in postmodern society. Hocking, in his historiographies of statistics, argues that the quantification of the individual through statistical analysis changed the way we think about ourselves in society. He believes that statistical studies of populations generated a discourse about a whole. Conversely, the studies themselves have caused the individuals to categorize themselves. However, these categories are really exterior to the society or individual. This process serves to reinforce class structure, the supposedly objective nature of capitalism or markets, and, finally, the illusion of individual as consumer. Neil Postman (1992) calls this the "calculable person" (p. 138), one who knows his or her value as calculated by an external, refereed source. This clearly transcends the functionalized self described in the last chapter.

Claude Levi-Strauss explained social unity in terms of communication. Members of a society are not, in his mind, drawn toward a single belief, or center, as was the position of Durkheim. He believed that members are "bonded together by a perpetual weave and shuttle of transactions" (Harland, 1987, p. 25). Exchanges, whether they be exchanges of marriage or kinship, etc., explained the nature of community. This shift in locus of influence changed social thought in two ways. First, it emphasized the value of communication as core to social structure. Second, it argued and illustrated that the more important factor in defining community was the relationship between families and not within them.

At a social level, then, Levi-Strauss saw these differences between families based on communication patterns and rules put down by family to family interactions form a social system. These rules then formulate existing actions. This overlay of rules forms a grid. The grid not only classifies what is important in a community, but it also, and more importantly, makes communication possible. The grid is used to decipher information. The grid also helps one contrast and compare and, therefore, make decisions. In this way identity is not that one perceives oneself as a member of a community, but they interpret their membership in a community. This is a subtle way of saying that communication is membership.

Foucault adopted the idea of grids as a means to describe the power of industrial modern grids to both individuate and totalize. For example, he saw census enumerations as an individualization technique within a totalization procedure. First, he believed that "grids" of statistical social analysis created, not just a new individual, but the very idea of an individual. There was no individual until the self thought about how it fit into the larger picture. Consequently, once one begins to think about oneself as an individual, one must think more about the notion of the social. At one level, Foucault agrees with Baudrillard about the transformation of the individual into marketable product. In another way, Foucault's idea of individuation within totalization chimes with the aforementioned idea of simultaneous implosion and explosion. As we individuate, our society becomes much more complex. The need for additional grids becomes an invaluable aid.

Further, Foucault (1970) believed that as the types of grids increase, we are increasingly pressured to distinguish ourselves with more and more grids. The result is an increasingly fragmented person, owing all allegiances to many and none to a few. In agreement with Baudrillard, Foucault argues that the individual now spends most of his time fitting oneself into the market. This action commodifies the self and, to a degree, makes for a fragmented (Foucault, 1970), schizophrenic (Baudrillard, 1983a), or saturated (Gergen, 1991) self. Baudrillard goes even further to say that people have mistaken the "map" for the landscape. In other words, we mistake a very artificial mediated grid for the real one.

We are probably more aware of the social grid than ever before. This is due to having more information about the society in which we live more than ever before. But more and more we are made aware of where we stand on the grid. We are packaged and sold by the mass media, marketers, and researchers. We come to know our own demographics and to which audience(s) we belong. One might argue that this influence is so strong that the audience grid has become a large part of the social grid or even supplanted the social grid.

Audiences are not naturally occurring phenomena. They are not even the gathering of people in either a controlled or helter-skelter situation. They do not "travel" together or just come together because something has been built (build it and they will come). Audiences are the product of discourse about them and by them. Audiences are discursive subjects. They are nonexistent before they are conceptualized by a market, history, or themselves.

Audiences are, it is easily argued, too large for their members and researchers to have direct experience. They must be told who they are, by not only their would be producers, but also themselves. To a large extent in our era, they are constructs of research and become how they are described. An audience is "not fact but a set of pragmatics" (Anderson, 1996, 75). It is true that audiences, once constructed, structure and are structured by their discourse. In a way this also echoes Fredric Jameson's idea that cognitive maps exist between the real realms of the actual people and the content of message.

Audiences even in the classical sense were individuals who came together in a social gathering and interacted with one another, as well as with the author of the work, to see or hear. The author had a first-hand relationship with the audience. The audience understood the motivations of the author. However, the nature of his or her content changed the nature of that audience as it created some sort of discourse less than and greater to in many ways the actual content of the message. But because of the proximity of the relationship between the author and the audience we imagine that the classical relationship was free of a separate interpretable discourse. In some ways, this classical notion of audience/author relationship has carried over to contemporary notions of audience. However, the contemporary viewer has a romantic vision market of the author/audience relationship that is not true.

Obviously, however, the author/audience relationship is and has become much more complex. Part of the complexity is a result of holding the classical view. The viewer imagines a personal relationship, but evolution of audience has also created a more complex relationship that is much stronger and engrained. One of the most important results of that evolution is the shift from author/audience, the classical view, to text/reader. The first thing one recognizes is the limitations placed on both the transmitter and the receptor. The relationship is medium and individual, not creator and created.

However, the resultant text/reader relationship is much more than the influence of the contemporary medium and the rise of individualism. The problem is that the text is imagined as separated from the author and freely interpreted by every individual. The emphasis on the reader permits a reader as functionalized by the technology, not by a human relationship with an author.

To illustrate how this has come to be, we must first look at the development of the contemporary view of the audience. James Anderson (1996) writes about the construction of the audience. He says that the concept of audience is inextricably bound up in the construction of the individual. This is true, but the individual has also historically become less aware of the structuring of the self by the social process and has become self-absorbed.

This is not a natural evolution of the concept of the individual. All of the philosophical constructs that are used by audience analysts assume that there is some degree of free agency. Theories reach the public through the discourse about their place in the market. The theories of free agency assume an accessible reality, authentic choices in the reality, and reason. The new free agency is usually not presented as being tempered by social, political, and economic forces.

Anderson describes four strains of thinking about free agency. I will only add that they are tied to an evolution based on the strengthening of external forces at the behest of the weaken knowledge of the self. These strains are mutations of one another. All emphasize the need for social construction.

First in Anderson's strains are the "cognitivists, who emphasize internal structures and can be seen as viewing the individual as an archive site—a repository of the processes of socialization" (p. 77). Analysts know the person as represented in the schema. The person is a place of expression.

Sociologists and culturalists, on the other hand, emphasize the external forces on the individual. The external forces submerge the individual who is known only by his or her submission or rebellion. Analysts define emancipatory impulses sometimes change the social or cultural structures.

The third view is the structuralist perspective. The individual is an "address where the outcomes of organism, community, and language are materialized in the fundamental structures of human action" (p. 77). Analysts see history as the analysand. Individuals in radical structuralism (e.g., Foucault) believe that the idea of the individual is completely erased by a historical discourse.

Poststructuralists argue a stronger view of free agency. The individual is action oriented, knowledgeable agent. However, this general belief by the individual overshadows the very real social, cultural, political, and economic structures.

I believe the self is overdetermined in this way and that the poststructuralists have a clear view of the contemporary melieu. The individual overcompensates for the self in an attempt to create his or her own structures. Obviously, the result is failure, leaving the individual schizophrenic or at least left with a set of unrelated, seemingly interchangeable meanings of self.

The philosophies mentioned above impact the way audiences are construct through discourse. The following is a review of the various views of practical audience construction. The first major category is the author's construct. The second major category is the construct created by the market or academic researcher. The latter is more pertinent to the present research.

The first type of audience is the formal audience (see Anderson, 1996). The formal audience is the audience directly addressed by the author. One kind of formal audience constructed by the writer is the encoded audience. This is the audience that everyone recognizes whether they include themselves or not. It is the recognizable "they" that the good writer always writes for—those who are reading. The other kind of formal audience is the analytic audience. This audience construct is based in assumptions that critics and scholars make before they critique a piece or study a population. Taste assumptions that the critic makes create the assumption of their existence and representativeness. The categorical decisions that a scholar must make also bias the frame within which the picture is painted.

The second type of audience is a direct creation of the audience analysts. The result is the empirical audiences. The first kind of empirical audience is the transcendental audience. This audience is defined by historically developed categories of audiences. For example, the adult audience of movie ratings is defined as eighteen years-of-age and older. This is indeed arbitrary. However, the category is functionally equivalent to any other. Adults are eighteen years-of-age and older and the eighteen years-of-age and older are adults. dental categories can come about in two major ways. The transcend ences can be more specifically the result of sampling protocols su used in market analysis. In this case, they are called aggregate audi categories arise from social discourse surrounding the discussion of or create the category, such as the category of "adult" arising fro over sexuality and obscenity, then the transcendental audience is referred to as the surrogate audience.

Ethnographic research has helped spawn a new audience most closely associated with the postmodern audience. The situated audience comes in many varieties, all of which stress the individual in everyday situations embedded in social action. For instance, the strategic audience is one that acts within interpretive strategies. The actor is always acting as a member of and on behalf of an interpretive community. They are always deciding how they are to interpret texts and how the community is to interpret the message. The latter is exported to the community in daily discussions based implicitly or explicitly on the content. Engaged audiences use the text as a sign of membership in a group. These communities are more likely to identify with the text and are highly dependent on knowing the others in the membership to help support the continuance of the text. An extreme engaged audience is called the emergent audience. They produce text in social action. Their action often mimics what they have seen of television. This is sort of a play of intertextuality between mass media in real life.

The most important word in the last several sentences is "text." In an attempt to emphasize the agent in the mass media process, the proponents of the ethnographic approach have enabled a viewer free of social constraints. However, on the way, the viewer has become a function of the mass media, a reader of texts. The person is functionalized. The viewer, which has its own semantic baggage, is now the reader who assumes that everyone reads the same things and that choice in reading involves reading or not. The fallacy of using the word "text" is that the dominant medium of the day is not a text. It should go without saying that television is not a text, not a linear, read thing. The use of "text" is primarily the result of method driving theory, just as the empiricists were guilty of. Scholars armed with tools to analyze texts decided to apply them elsewhere, transforming television to text and viewers to readers.

Audiences have never been real. Audiences are fictive. They are varying fictions created by researchers and writers. More than ever before, however, "audiences" have access to "audiences" as descriptive. Therefore, audiences are unlike they have ever been before. First, they believe they have a stable definition of themselves. Second, they have developed an unquestioning trust in the description. Third, because they are concrete and so accessible they believe that they have ultimate control. If one knows a mirror cannot lie, they not only trust it, but know that they control how they look. This creates a cybernetic viewer one who sees himself as the message sender and the medium as the feedback.

Consumption as "Non-Language Logic"

What happens to logic when an individual is primarily defined as an audience member? If language is personal, then there is no language of the system of signs. But is there a logic? The answer is probably yes. The logic is one of contradiction and confusion, however. Baudrillard suggests that the system of categories (needs and status) is distinctly not a language.

But "objects work as categories of objects which, in tyrannical fashion, define categories of people—they police meaning, and the signification they engender are rigidly controlled" (191). Therefore, the categories act as structure that masquerades as a logical system and a vector toward a sense of a social order.

Meaning is determined by a self-referential system of signifiers. Consumption is not use value, but the consumption of signs. Signs are consumed primarily through advertising. Through objects, each individual searches out his or her place in an order. The function of commodities is not just to meet individual needs, but also to relate the individual to the social order. Consumption is a system of exchange. Commodities are goods to think with in a semiotics system that precedes the individual, as does any language. There is no self-contained individual, there are only means of using the social system. Language is the social system that is common to all of us.

The consumption model and language meet here and produce a society that believes that consumption produces society and that language produces meaning. As a result culture is flattened. Anything that we can speak of is culture. Obviously that which everyone can talk about is the lowest common denominator of culture. The result is a flat and undefinable culture, which does not discriminate between high and low or popular culture. Lines of taste are erased. Taste becomes a useless concept as something that makes us different and unique. Taste is reduced to one ubiquitous mass that we know or don't (obviously, we believe that we all know it).

The language is created in the following process. First, the mass media generate a world of simulations which is immune to rationalist critique. Second, the mass media present an excess of information and they do so in a manner that excludes response by the recipients. Third, this simulated reality has no referent, no ground, no source. It operates outside of a logic of representation. However, the masses have to make it a language of sense-making—a system that stands for itself (floor wax = love).

Society is reduced to decentered individuals, as words in a sentence read in random order. In the explosion of meaning, we believe that we are more particular in naming things, to the point where we have named them absolutely and the things become the name. This opens the door for two effects: 1) Technologizing the word, in which we talk about things being the function of technology. People in this model only function as users; 2) Those who aren't users are marginalized, not just outside on account of race, religion, etc., but outside the new human being—the functional one.

At this point in his argument in *The Systems of Objects*, Baudrillard uses the concept of "brand" to describe the post structural system of objects.

> Brand . . . sums up the prospect for a "language" of consumption rather well . . . Every product worthy of the name has a brand which may sometimes even become generic (e.g. Frigidaire). The brand's primary function is to designate a product; its secondary function is to mobilize emotional connotations (p. 191).

Brand loyalty is an emotional attachment to a social meaning. It is the psychological component of every product. It is the only way that a product speaks to us and we speak to the product. This is the language—the willingness to speak to ourselves as embodied in the sign of the brand. It is language of mere signals; brand loyalty can never, therefore, be more than conditioned reflex of manipulated emotions. Likewise, brands change and loyalty is constantly changing just like emotions. This limitation of an emotional language points back to the illusion of free choice.

Free choice is a censor. As we are increasingly frustrated with this system of contradictions and limitations, we restrict ourselves to fewer and fewer personalizing attributes. This censorship inhibits our drive to be different but at the same time to be in search of new and better categories. Individuals define themselves through their objects. "Coherence is achieved through the institution of a combinatorial system or repertoire—a language that is functional, certainly, but symbolically and structurally immiserated" (p. 195).

The Current State of Affairs in Media Effects Research

New methods have had a hand in the development of the shift in the paradigm. The so-called cognitive revolution was the result of methodological growing pains, as well as theoretical ones. Black box surveys and experiments were de-emphasized. Longitudinal data were emphasized along with supplemental data including those from content analyses, quasi-experiment, and focus groups (Beniger, 1987).

Limited effects were warded off by more subtle articulations of research models that included analyses of the mass media frame and the audience cognitions. Critical/cultural theory can be seen as an influence on this revised model. James Beniger (1987) highlights three theories that "revived" strong effects: agenda setting (McCombs and Shaw, 1972), spiral of silence (Noelle-Neumann, 1974), and cultivation analysis (Gerbner and Gross, 1976). These models have more recently spawned other theories such as framing, meaning theory, and media dependency theory.

I will follow the discussion of these theories by presenting critical/cultural theory as introduced by British cultural theorists. They serve to question how we look at the current state of mass media effects, just as other challengers to previous dominant paradigms, but to show how critical/cultural theory shapes the self.

Agenda Setting

Agenda setting is best described as the "mass media don't tell us what to think, but what to think about." In other words, the public's agenda, what it believes are the most important issues of the day, is correlated with the amount of news about the same issues. It rejects mass media effects at the behavior and emotional levels in favor of a focus on the cognitive domain.

Maxwell McCombs and Donald Shaw (1972) initiated the study of agenda setting effects. They found that what is reported in the mass media has high salience among the public. McCombs (2005) writes that agenda setting works because of the old scientific principle that "Nature hates a vacuum" (p. 53). More specifically, he believes that people don't want to live in a "cognitive vacuum" (p. 53) and that we strive to know the world around us. However, we do have choice based on personal relevance of an issue or issues. He continues: "Conceptually, an individual's need for orientation is defined in terms of two lower-order concepts, relevance and uncertainty, whose roles occur sequentially. Relevance is the initial defining condition of need for orientation" (54).

This finding set off a flurry of studies over the past thirty years. As a matter of fact, agenda setting has become the most studied mass media phenomenon in its short history. The research shows not only strong evidence of the existence of the agenda setting function but also strong effects at the cognitive level. When combined with social factors including education, occupation, and geographic location, researchers have shown that the effects of the mass media's agenda on an individual's agenda are quite strong. (Weaver, Graber, McCombs, and Eyal, 1981)

Over the years a more comprehensive model of agenda setting has been built.

Consequences of Agenda Setting

MEDIA AGENDA   PUBLIC AGENDA

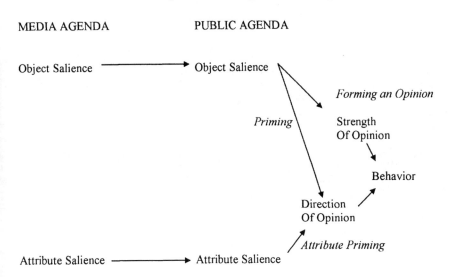

Figure 6.1.

The top part of the model is the original idea in that we see how the mass media agenda sets the public agenda based on the salience of the object or issue. The issue is amplified through "selection, emphasis, exclusion and elaboration" (McCombs, 87). McCombs labels this attribute salience. Both attribute and object salience work together to prime opinions that affect behavior.

By including attribute salience in the model, McCombs is attempting to do at least two things. First, how a story is or not presented cannot be separated from the salience of the topic in determining the effects of the message on behavior. This is done for a second reason, which is to oppose theorists who focus only on what he calls attribute salience or what others call framing. Framing theory relies merely on the bias of presentation to explain coercive effects. Framing will be discussed later.

McCombs clearly points out how agenda setting is different from the preceding theories. First, he believes all "effects" follow cognitive elaboration. Not only do all others follow but individuals have choice based on relevance to themselves.

More directly, McCombs writes:

> the idea of powerful media effects as expressed in the concept of agenda setting was a better explanation for the salience of issues on the public agenda than was the concept of selective perception, which was the keystone in the idea of minimal mass media consequences . . .
>
> Agenda setting is not a return to the bullet or hypodermic theory of all-powerful media effects. Nor are members of the audience regarded as automatons waiting to be programmed by the news media. But agenda setting does not assign a central role to the news media initiating items for the public agenda . . .
>
> In contrast, the concept of selective perception locates the central influence within the individual and stratifies media content according to its compatibility with an individual's existing attitude and opinions (p. 6).

Agenda setting research is important in the furthering of the notion that social cognition is an important framework within which to study the mass media's influence. By using a framework that included the mass media within an individual's social cognition, not merely one that influences one's social cognition.

The self's cognition as viewed through agenda setting is a thin map, not a multilevel decisionmaking tool. The shallow map is drawn by the mass media. And because there is no proof of a link between one's agenda and one's actions, the map is just a map. Baudrillard might say here that the map has been mistaken for the reality. The self is a shallow, mass media saturated (Gergen, 1994) one. And needless to say, the self in this condition is operating on a simulacrum of created by the illusion of the cognitive map.

At the same time, because the agenda settings research program also sets out to argue that people don't get what they want but are told what they want, it unveils a self that is under the illusion that it gets what it wants. Consequently, the self packages itself for the mass media market. The self prepares itself by shaping its desirable attributes, believing that the mass media subsequently delivers when indeed those attributes have already been manipulated by the mass media market. This was true of the last paradigm but in this case there are significant differences. Under agenda setting, the self delivers itself, not as a member of a target group, but as an individual, a self that wants to be unique like everyone else. The self has a more direct connection with the mass media and therefore does not join groups, or that is what we believe, to be delivered to the market. In the end, the self fragments itself in order to be delivered directly to different mass media market segments.

The model presented here is also a strong effects model. However, the agenda setting model turns the early strong effects model on its head in that strong effects are now the result of the self giving itself to the market through a increasingly deep relationship with information technology. What deeper relationship can we have than to believe that our map of the world is determined by the mass media. It is as if we see our cognition on the small screen. The postmodern self is increasingly revealing itself at this stage.

The Spiral of Silence

Elizabeth Noelle-Neumann (1973, 1980, 1993) argues that mass media effects lie in the relationship between public opinion and self-perceived notions of how and where one's own opinion fits. The process is characterized by cumulation, ubiquity, and consonance. Cumulation refers to the recurrence of certain themes and messages over time. Ubiquity is the reinforcement of those themes and messages through a ubiquitous mass media. And consonance is the agreement between various types of mass media and the narrowing of opinions covered over time.

Consequently, individuals find themselves not just embedded in an environment of public opinion, but a specific kind that she calls the spiral of silence. It works like this: in addition to forming opinions, individuals form impressions of overall public opinion. They then see themselves and assess where they are in relation to the majority and minorities. If they are in the majority, they want public opinion to change to their side. If they are in the minority, they remain silent. As one then senses their continued exclusion, they become even more reticent about their idea. At the same time, their lack of "voice" weakens their side's opposition and strengthens the majority.

The theory has mixed support. Dominie Lasorsa (1991) found that outspokenness was affected by age, education, income, level of self-efficacy, attention to political news media, and certitude to one's position, but not to personal relevance or general mass media use. On the other hand, Michael Salwen, Carolyn Lin, and Frances Matera found that willingness to speak out is relate to perception of national public opinion and perception of national news coverage more than perception of local opinion or local mass media coverage of an issue.

Psychologically, fear of exclusion or isolation governs one's actions and gives strength to the dominant opinion and, because it is the center of public opinion formation, strength, and endurance, to the media. Anderson (1996) writes, "An analysis of the assumptions follows along the constructiveist/objectivist route: Social realities are functionally equivalent to material realities, and our engagement of either is trustworthy. The individual is a social animal governed by the need for social cohesion and the fear of isolation" (p. 214).

Noelle-Neumann says that individuals have a sixth sense that monitors public opinion. As a self this illustrates the postmodern self's emotional subjectivity as one that is unmindful, anti-intellectual, and personal. The self operating on this sixth sense is unmindful of real sources of knowledge. The sense is not what ideas and identity are but where one's emotions lie on the field of public opinion. The idea that there is no real decisionmaking process going is certainly anti-intellectual. Public opinion as all encompassing and powerful makes for a world in which no other power or logic is wielded. And the self is a very personal one forming an identity based upon identity politics, another hallmark of the postmodern. In other words guided in every aspect of life based on where it fits in based on how it identifies with issues and not real politics as a whole.

Cultivation Hypothesis

The cultivation hypothesis is derived from the notion that television is the storyteller of current times. The storyteller tells us who we have been who we are and who we could be. Storytelling itself is central to all cultural systems. The storyteller cultivates us into our culture and teaches us what we share. Stories make life bearable. James Anderson (1996) points out that stories are not narratives. Stories are a screen of reality that "hides the true face of reality" (p. 211).

In more direct terms, cultivation explains that those who watch more television are more likely to develop a world that is more closely related to the world of television. It is not arguable that television's world is extremely different than the real world. It intends to be different. Therefore, heavy viewers end up with a distorted reality when compared to light viewers.

This type of empirical data is used to support the "mean world hypothesis." Heavy viewers tend to believe that the real world is a meaner place than it really is because television's world is. Therefore, heavy viewers are more likely to participate in real life in a variety of ways. In order to test this George Gerbner et al. (1986) tested the relationship between first- and second-order beliefs. First-order beliefs are those about the real world. Second-order effects concern extrapolation from those beliefs. Concerning the mean world theory, the relationship would be one of belief that the world is mean (first-order) and inaction (second order). Correlations between first- and second-order are weak (Hawking and Pingree, 1990).

The outcomes can vary for certain social groups. First, heavy viewers' distorted cultural notions may override reality. This is called mainstreaming. More specifically, mainstreaming explains that heavy viewers will be less likely to see variation in ideas or characteristics. Heavy viewers may also be more vulnerable if faced with content that resonates with something in their life. When faced with something that is part of their distorted reality, the heavy viewers will reinforce and possibly heighten their actions with those acceptable in television's world.

For example, mainstreaming occurs when heavy viewers in both high and low income groups share the same views on crime. However, light viewers in both high and low income groups do not share the same views as each other. The low income group shares the views of heavy viewers, while the high income group does not. Mainstreaming predicts that in some comparisons social variables override television's effect. Resonance occurs in comparing male and female heavy viewers and their views on crime. Females generally resonate more with vulnerability to crime and, therefore, have a more exaggerated view of it than males.

Cultivation still has fans, especially through the establishment of the extended cultivation hypothesis. Douglas McLeod et al. (1995) believe that cultivation is strong when types of shows or genres are isolated. Interestingly enough, his comes on the heels of the birth of reality crime programs. Support has been shown for cultivation effects of local news in the case of crime reporting. However, Gerbner and his associates have continually rejected the invocation of the term "cultivation analysis" in these studies because they do not follow the logic set out by the theory, i.e., that television as an entirety is a culture or reality.

Gerbner was very concerned with mass media education. He believed that proper engagement of reality, televised or otherwise, could be taught. This strongly echoes the purpose of critical theory in the age of the Frankfort School. From this, Anderson points out:

> this position offers the clear view of the conjunctive model of the individual at work. The individual is the site of the materialization of the influence of television's stories. Television is a cultural lever that moves us to a common, albeit distorted, set of beliefs. resisting television's power to shape reality requires special training (p. 211).

Although cultivation analysis finds that television's direct effect is too weak to moderate, there is consistent support for the hypothesis as modified thorough mainstreaming and resonance. More importantly, no other model or research project has had as much public involvement through mass media reportage. From the early days the research garnered funding from the AMA, the Administration on Aging, NSF, and various other agencies. Needless to say, the findings were bound to gain some attention. Even today, part of the analysis, the measure of violence on television, is reported wide and far. So, therefore, exposure in a sense makes it an even stronger theory in the public's eye than it is, especially when other theories are not shown as competing.

Gerbner's cultivated self does not make distinctions between high and low culture. This is one of the tenants of postmodernism. Television cultivates a large portion of the population. If Gerbner is right, everything that is televised is neither high or low culture by virtue of merely being on television. Some people may only watch high culture on PBS but if it is great amounts of PBS, then the viewer is cultivated to the same world as someone who watches nothing but reality programming. In either case, the lines are removed in a world put forth by cultivation analysis.

The personal relationship is clearly evident in the use of television hours watched as the center of the cultivation hypothesis and mean world theorizing. The relationship is even more concentrated than in previous theories.

What is probably more important for a postmodern prospective is that a cultural simulacrum is built for people who watch great amounts of television. It is not necessarily a distorted version of another reality, but a whole new one that exists no place else. That place, as Gertrude Stein once said about Oakland,

California, "has no there there." In postmodern terms, the place that television exists has no stable meta-narratives, therefore it creates a culture without logical, moral ties. The lack of meta-narratives is contributed to the lack of reference. This can be evidenced at any time by viewing what is one pastiche after another of emotions without any or clear references to any thing other than to itself.

Framing

Erving Goffman's (1974) initially defined a frame as a "principle of organization which governs events—at least social ones—and our subjective involvement in them" (p. 11). Frames enable us to "locate, perceive, identify, and label a seemingly infinite number of concrete occurrences" (p. 21). Frames are used to make sense of the world.

The debate concerning framing theory today focuses on what or who determines frames. Some theorists see framing as as a consciously used journalistic tool. For example, Oscar Gandy (2001) explains that frames "are used purposively to direct attention and then to guide the processing of information so that the preferred reading of the facts come to dominate public understanding" (p. 365). Kathleen Jamieson and Paul Waldman (2002) believe that frames are "the structures underlying the depict ions that the public reads, hears, and watches" (p. xii). Framing takes place when journalists "select some aspects of a perceived reality and make them more salient in a communicating text" (Entman, 1993, p. 52). By attempting to organize experiences for readers, journalists "highlight some bits of information about an item that is the subject of communication, thereby elevating them in salience" (p. 53).

Others see framing as more politically based. Paul D'Angelo (2004) argues, journalists provide "interpretive packages" of the positions of parties who have a political investment in an issue. In so doing, journalists "both reflect and add" to what William Gamson and Andre Mogdiliani (1987) call the "issue culture" of a topic. D'Angelo argues that frames limit our political awareness, hamstring activists, and "set parameters for policy debates not necessarily in agreement with democratic norms." Journalists select sources because they are credible, and believe that even a long-standing frame has value because it contains "a range of viewpoints that is potentially useful" to our understanding of an issue (p. 877).

Still some others see framing as more of an unconscious activity better defined by the journalists work environment. For example, Ron Bishop (2006) writes, "Frames are more a product of a story's unruliness and the reporter's need to meet deadlines than of a journalist flexing a particular ideology." True to their job routines, reporters covered "the event, not the condition; the conflict, not the consensus; the fact that 'advances the story,' not the one that explains it" (Gitlin, p. 122). Reporters pay significant attention to spokespeople who "most closely matched prefabricated images of what an opposition leader should look and sound like: theatrical, bombastic, and knowing and inventive in the ways of packaging messages" (p. 154) for maximum mass media exposure. The group's goals and ideas were less important because they made for less than compelling stories.

This drive to find compelling stories is echoed in Jack Lule's contention that news is composed of what Lule believes are "enduring, abiding stories" (Lule, 2001, p. 3). In covering what goes on in the world, journalists tap "a deep but nonetheless limited body of story forms and types." This reliance on certain story forms is no surprise, writes Lule, given our love for and dependence on stories. "We understand our lives and our world through story," he argues (p. 3).

Perhaps more important for our journey, Lule contends that familiar myths—"the great stories of humankind" (p. 15)—regularly come to life in news reporting. Lule defines myth as "a sacred, social story that draws from archetypal figures to offer exemplary models for human life" (p. 17). Myths empower society to express its "prevailing ideals, ideologies, values, and beliefs." They are, Lule writes, "models of social life and models for social life" (p. 15). Myths are not evident in every news story, as Lule cautions, but in many instances journalists draw upon "the rich treasure trove of archetypal stories" to revisit those shared stories that help us make sense of the world in which we live.

Lule's analysis of news produced seven of what he calls "master myths" found in news: the victim, whose life is abruptly altered by "the randomness of human existence"; the scapegoat, deployed in stories to remind us of "what happens to those who challenge or ignore social beliefs"; the hero, there to remind us that we have the potential for greatness; the good mother, who offers us "a model of goodness in times when goodness may seem in short supply" (p. 24); the trickster, a crafty figure who usually ends up bringing "on himself and others all manner of suffering," thanks to his crude, boorish behavior; the other world, which enables us to feel good about our way of life by contrasting it, sometimes starkly, with ways of life elsewhere; and the flood, in which we see the "destruction of a group of people by powerful forces," often because they have "strayed from the right path" (p. 25).

All of the types of frame analysis deal with cognition from the producer's point of view. In general, cognitive maps of storytelling are meant to resonate with an audience, not necessarily to attract an audience but to maintain an audience. Here, I have chosen the word "maintain" carefully to bring about the sense of audience-making as spoken about earlier. The question is, however, have frames or the process of framing changed framing itself? Framing itself does not answer this question. A good history of journalism, such as *Discovering the News* by Michael Schudson, might. As journalism became professionalized and scientized, I believe we would be able to apply my thesis at the level of news.

Meaning Theory

Uses and gratification's methods and longitudinal studies (Beniger, 1987) had a great latent effect on the recent turns in communication research. The studies provided a reality check to the assumptions of the mass society theory. Some of Blumer's ideas have resurfaced in the form of social learning theory (Bandura). In mass media research, meaning theory was one of the new ideas to emerge.

In meaning theory, the individual is perceived as a form of behavior from mass media content. The individual then judges the usefulness. If the individual decides to use the behavior future use will depend on its actual success or failure.

Media may also have an effect on our cognitive maps in general. The mass media may give new, additional meanings or reduce meanings that we already hold. In meaning theory, we then act based on the level of meaning that the act may have for us.

The propositions of both theories are cognitive in nature. Cognitive maps are not the basis of action, but are the tools used to predetermine or mediate thought to action. In modeling theory the individual models events within a conceptual structure before acting on them. In other words, the person bases actions on maps that enable him or her to assess behavior to some degree. In meaning theory, the map is determined in large part by mass media events. Therefore action is based not on a rational thought process, but a more mentalistic process.

These theories have given us better descriptive model of individual differences in mass media use. In many cases the mass media have a powerful effect. In this way the limited effects paradigm was weakened. Theoretically, these modeling theories have taken us full circle, back to a vulgar behaviorist (mentalistic) paradigm. Although choice seems to be of utmost importance, as revealed in greater attention to the individual, the action of the individual is set based on a socially constructed set of meanings.

It seems that although these models do not reduce meaning or action to some predetermined demographic or psychographics variables, more subtle determiners have been found. Media shapes those precursors. This leads to another problem that was also true of uses and gratifications. If indeed mass media makes meaning, then what is the use of studying people for the meaning? In other words, a tautology has been created when mass media effects are studied in this way. The interesting turn here is that once we would only have to study subjects for mass media effects; now, if the meaning theory is correct, we should only have to study the mass media itself. It's us.

Media Systems Dependency Theory

Media systems dependency theory (DeFleur and Ball-Rokeach, 1989) develop what they call an "ecological theory" (p. 302). The model is organic in that it examines both micro (the viewer) and macro (the mass media systems) social systems. They follow the normal tenets of general systems theory stability, change, adaptation, meaning, and the individual. Interrelationships are emphasized at all levels.

They write:

> the media system is assumed to be an important part of the social fabric of modern society, and it is seen to have relationships with individuals groups, organizations and other social systems. These relationships may be conflict ridden, or cooperative; they may dynamic and changing or static and orderly. They also may range from being direct and powerful to being indirect or weak. Whatever the particulars of the relationship, it is the relationship that carries the burden of explanation (p. 309).

This all boils down to measuring dependencies of individuals to the mass media and media to individuals, media to media, individuals to individuals, individual to a particular medium, and so on. All of this leads to the understanding that "people construct their own media systems" (p. 309) based on their dependencies to individual media or the system in general. The process is easily understood by examining their model.

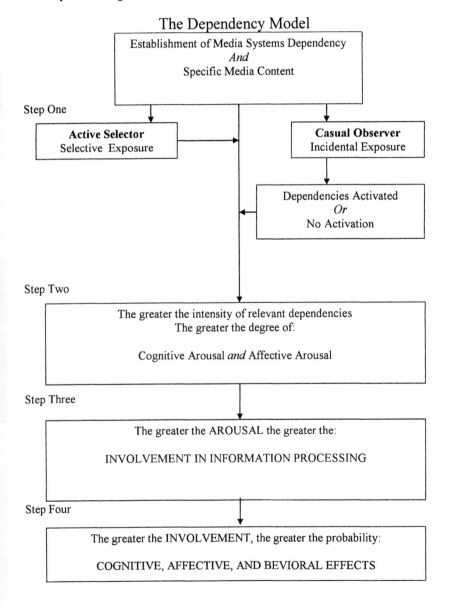

Figure 6.2.

The most important part of the model according to the authors, or at least the most interesting part to mass media effects scholars, is step one. What motivates a user to actively select a medium or information? How is dependency activated? Herein lies the heavy reliance on cognitive models. "Media system dependency theory envisions a cognitive psychological process that increases the likelihood of one's being affected by particular media content" (311).

This statement also suggests that not only are the researchers interested in direct, strong effects, but may even assume that they abound. Like meaning theory, media system theory gives us a picture of a self that carries more than a personal relationship with the mass media but suggests that the mass media are a part of our make-up. And although they do account for individual differences, they do point out that differences are as much a part of mass media choices as they are psychological motivations and goals.

Critical/Cultural Theory

Raymond Williams (1980) put his brand on critical theory by saying that all forms of contemporary critical theory are theories of consumption and that they ignore production. In Marxian terms, he was asserting that critical theory as it is used to critique culture was not studying the base as it related to the superstructure. Theory affected real life, then, as a contemporary person comprising him or herself as a product of of taste and sensibility. Taste being associated with one's like and sensibility with the notion of sensible choice. In his description of the relationship between a viewer and art, he positions the self as all critical in the choice of art. The contemporary self has been taught to look at art only as text and to ask himself "do I like it?", "how do I feel?", or "what effect does it have?" The viewer essentially erases production and the artist by asking him or herself these questions. And of course, art is reduced to that which can be consumed by an almighty consumer.

Williams calls for a "return" to the inclusion of production in the critique of art. Furthermore, he calls for a more sophisticated view of art through hegemony theory as a product, not of the state but of the superstructure. More particularly, he hopes for future cultural theory to understand residual and emergent views of production and interpretation.

Williams fathered what became known as British cultural theory. Eventually, the theory would mature and be recognized as the convergence of critical theory and poststructural theory. As Durham and Kellner write:

> the Birmingham Centre adopted a critical approach that, like the Frankfort School, but without some of the flaws, interpreted culture within society and situated the study of culture within the field of contemporary social theory and oppositional politics. . . . the Birmingham project paved the way . . . for a postmodern populist turn in cultural studies, which responds to a later stage of capitalism. Emphasis on consumption, on audience creation of meaning, on difference and heterogeneity, corresponds to the contemporary stage of global capitalism in which consumer soverenity is celebrated, more differences are

tolerated and marketed, and audiences are enjoined to embrace new products, technology, and produce novel identities (p. 96).

Here we see references to critical theory in two ways. First, is the reference to consumption and declining capitalism. Next is the education of the masses, all people, in the nature of messages. Poststructualism is addressed in its stand on polysemy and oppositional positions.

This is where British cultural studies enters to advanced Marx's position not only theoretically but also toward a greater explanation through an emphasis on mass media domination. One of their positions is that the mass media works with the dominant institutions in society. In this way the mass media emphasize what is "normal" and deemphasize what is outside the normal. The values of most social groups are not heard from or recognized. Much of the research in the British tradition examines the portrayal or lack thereof of groups that would be outside of the power class. The mass media is seen as "renewing, amplifying, and extending the existing pre dispositions that constitute the dominant culture, not creating them" (Curran et al., 1982, 14).

Stuart Hall is the most important scholar in the British cultural studies movement. His critique includes influences by Antonio Gramsci's hegemony theory and Louis Althusser's concept of the production of dominant ideologies by an autonomous mass media. For Hall the mass media serve the ruling class by creating ideological struggle. The news, for example, creates a viewpoint by evoking public opinion and attributing it to government and other power institutions.

Hall's primary level of analysis focuses on the individual level for the purposes of hypothesizing to the structural equation. He positions the individual as a reader reading a text. This is a very important turn in theory, the notion of a reader and his text. As has been said, once we position an individual as a reader, we seemingly give him free choice. We also reduce television to content that is to be interpreted by the reader. As I've already stated, I believe that this view gives too much credit to television. It is not literature in that it is relatively apolitical, yet not non-ideological. But in any case, despite Hall's use of these terms, he still ties the act of reading to a political phenomenon that is more than personal.

In his method, Hall examines what he calls "preferred readings" in the mass media. This is the study of readings produced by particular social situations in which the individual positions him or herself. Dominant readings are those whose social situations are in favor of the preferred reading. Negotiated readings inflect the preferred reading from their social position. Oppositional readings are from a position of the conflict with the preferred reading. The mass media then are in what Hall calls a "site of struggle." The site of the struggle includes all positions not in the presentation (i.e., representing all viewpoints) but in the allowance for interpretation. The site begins and ends with a meaningless struggle and conformity with the values of the state.

The British cultural studies view follows Gramsci lead then in rejecting economic determinism. His humanist view places ideology as independent of economics. The dominant class uses ideology to project as way of seeing the world that is common sense and natural. Hegemony is the ever changing process by which the ruling class reminds the subordinate class of itself and its subordination to the ruling class. More precisely, hegemony is the process within the "site of struggle" in which the individual is stupefied by the contradictions between not so common common sense that he has learned and his social experience. Gramsci would probably agree that the mass media is a powerful center where these contradictions are worked out. The contradictions are not worked out among the classes. They are more likely to be further confused on a daily basis.

John Fiske (1992) looks even more closely at the individual and his confusion. He believes:

> The individual is produced by nature; the subject by culture. Theories of the individual concentrate on differences between people and explain these differences as natural. Theories of the subject, on the other hand, concentrate on people's common experiences in a society as being the most productive way of explaining who (we think) we are . . . The subject . . . is a social construction, not a natural one (p. 288).

This notion of the subject is Althusserian. It imagines an individual lacking self-consciousness. Ideological functions constitute an individual. Ideological state apparatuses include the mass media. The apparatuses structure the person to fit a given culture. This is often called structural Marxism and holds the same assumptions that the structural linguists believed that language and social events structure our everyday lives. Fiske differs from Althusser in that Althusser would have not allowed individuals to resist the dominant ideology. Fiske sees an individual who is molded by the mass media through his interaction with it. Therefore, the decision to interact is free choice. However, Fiske would agree that most of the individual's interactions are false and compliant to the dominant ideology.

Hall believes that the individual is situated as a consumer and the self is commodified. However, his mission is to free individual in two major ways. First is to understand cultural production in the mass media. This includes the technical infrastructure, relations of production, and frameworks of knowledge. He stresses that the individual must understand the means of production and how they create discursive products. This involves understanding of where story structures come from or how are they constructed in ways that then come prepackaged for the best audience understanding. And then, how does production add or subtract from the way the story is told? All of this is then couched in the web of mass media relationships and how they might affect the telling of the story.

Subsequently, understanding the encoding of messages is key to decoding the messages in the way of a semiologist. The individual viewer in Hall's mind can be taught to decode messages as an active viewer, not just in a uses and effects way and to merely pick and choose messages, but to be empowered with methods of interpretation. The process of decoding is the understanding of where the individual stands on a given set of messages. The individual has the option of decoding the dominant code, hegemonic, the one that the mass media delivers as a preferred meaning or intent.

This is not to say that the individual is blind to the polysemic nature of the code and can apply other codes. Individuals may apply a negotiable code in which an audience. A trained audience can negotiate the dominant hegemonic position using "adaptive or oppositional elements" (p. 128). Or the individual may understand the dominant code and follow it but not behave based upon it. Lastly, an oppositional code may be expressed by substituting ones own individual meanings, class meanings, ethnic meanings, etc. For example, every time George W. Bush says "freedom," "liberty," or "democracy" in any form, I substitute expanding market control.

Hall addresses the the strength of the use of semiotics as well as the weakness of existing communication theory in his best known work.

> Beginnings and endings have been announced in communication research before, so we must be cautious. But there seems some ground for thinking that a new and exciting phase in so-called audience research, of a new kind, may be opening up. At either end of the communication chain the use of the semiotic paradigm promises to dispel the lingering behaviorism which has dogged mass media research for so long, especially in its approach to content. Though we know the television programme is not a behavioural input, like a tap on the kneecap, it seems to have been almost impossible for traditional researchers to conceptualize the communicative process without lapsing into one or other variant of low-lying behaviorism. We know, as Gerbner has remarked, that representations of violence on the tv screen "are not violence, but messages about violence," but we have continued to research the question of violence, for example, as if we were unable to comprehend this epistemological distinction.

I believe that Hall has hit the problem on the head here, in that we are stuck in a rut but the rut is a historical view of the self and possibly a rut in which the self is realized. What I would like to add is that, for communication research's sake, we should be, as I am attempting, studying why we choose to study things in the matter that we study them.

The active viewer mirrors the aforementioned view of the individual, especially the male portable viewer. Television in this view frees the viewer to learn and interpret the world in his or her own way. If one chooses not to watch it is because the content does not function in the life of the individual—it is not useful. It also harmonizes with the critical view in that the viewer could be free if he or she were critical of the content.

The new strong effects model is carried in the language of the viewer. The viewer seeks out identity from greater and greater distances, both physical and mental. This is a self that is "tele"—at a distance. This teleself is his own brand that names itself from further and further distances. In some ways, I envision the Nike person. Nike doesn't exist anywhere. Nike is, at best, a contract for the lowest priced items. Nike exist only as a brand in the most extreme case. It is a name that, when attached, makes things much more important and, of course, expensive. This is that other worldly power of signs that float. In our case, the self can float as a sign now that it possesses the language of the media.

Agenda setting, cultivation analysis, and spiral of silence each paint a picture of an individual that neither is subject or object. In each case the media merely draw out what the individual already possesses. The individual has emotional antennae in search of pleasure. These pleasures construct a new emotional facade that is pure pastiche and a higher level of simulacrum.

Chapter Seven

Ferment of the Teleself: Releasing the Free Agent

In the first chapter, I introduced my favorite television program from the 1960s, called *Branded.* In the second, and last, season of the television program, Jason McCord meets, by chance, President Ulysses S. Grant. The president, knowing that McCord is a do-gooder and has lost his identity, makes him a spy. He is the perfect spy, an invisible voyeur, who even if discovered remains anonymous. Is the teleself a spy, a voyeur, or just someone who wants to remain anonymous?

At this point, all of the media effects discourses of the twentieth century have been folded into one another—the passive into the active, the active into the commodified, and all into the teleself.

In the first two steps the self concentrates on the content of the media. This was not because the content is so intriguing or powerful but because the technology remained a mystery concealed in a black box. Yet the mystery that surrounds the technology is intriguing. This enables the technology and the industry to reduce the individual to a subject upon which to test stimuli. Subjects in this way are very similar to one another. In other words, we believe we are more alike than we are different.

The active viewer is the result of an action model based on free agency. The free agent is an object, no longer a subject. As an object, the individual with fewer similarities to others is set free. In this way the individual is made up of marketable, segmentable attributes.

Next, the "viewer as reader" myth was created. Readers reading not just one program, because that is easily refuted and reduced to functional psychology. Readers in this case were reading a multitude of varying meanings. Readers took in what they needed and discarded what they didn't in order to develop a more marketable self. Surface maps, both early cognitive and programmatic, were taken and made representative of the reading experience. Readers, even more importantly, become defined by the audience to which they belong. Audiences are a simulacrum of marketers and academics.

The teleself is not a subject or object, a reader or interpreter. He or she integrates texts' marketable grids as they are of use for him or her. Individuals are seemingly completely aware that they are to change in a moment or roll with the tide to make a more marketable self. This hyperactive self turns on itself to package itself willingly for the good of the market.

In simple terms, the self has become postmodern and has nearly fulfilled all of the characteristics of the postmodernism (see Appendix for a discussion). Jameson (1983 and 1984) outlines six characteristics of postmodernism. They are: 1) a break with established and dominant forms; 2) the blurring of low and high culture distinctions; 3) depthlessness; 4) fragmentation or schizophrenia; 5) emotional subjectivity; and 6) a deep relationship with new technologies.

The first four have been fulfilled. The teleself has no set values or attributes and denies any tradition or at least ones that don't fit the moment. This happened early on as the media blurred the lines by "dumbing down" high culture and glorifying the popular, especially through the star system or celebrity culture. Of course, this is true because the postmodern self blurs all boundaries and replaces them with a depthlessness of the superficial marketplace, which is only made up of status signs and symbols. And as I wrote about in the last two chapters, the self can change its look at the drop of a hat based on market fragmentation.

The last two characteristics are illustrated in some contemporary research. Third-person effects is one and the media equation is the other. Both of these theories frame an otherliness in which the viewer is not even present. The self is represented as itself but as not being someone else and living through media as self-identification.

Third-Person Effects

The third-person effects hypothesis, as established by W. Phillips Davidson (1983), states that individuals will overestimate the attitudinal and behavioral effects that mass communicated messages have on individuals other than themselves. This is often referred to as the perceptual hypothesis. Because others are perceived as more vulnerable to messages, individuals question their possible behaviors.

The theory positions the individual as seeing almost everyone else not like themselves and as not being very discriminating when it comes to media messages. The theory then leads to the question of whether individuals, because of this particular view of other, may be more likely to want restriction on messages meant for individuals who are not like them, e.g., censorship of a particular type of music.

The self in the third-person effects hypothesis is an elitist who believes that only they have the self-awareness and free choice. We end up with a society of completely detached individuals because everyone is superior to everyone else. Identity is free floating, yet not in the other. In the other, identity is very strongly tied to television.

The theory paints a picture of the often suggested postmodern self that is schizophrenic. In general the self is not the subject, object, both, or even erased. The self is another person. This person is defined by worries about the other. The self worries that others are victims of media effects while the self is not. The self gains immunity, just as characters on reality shows. The theory also helps complete a postmodern self as it teases out the self as self-referential, one that is the baseline for all "normal" behavior, which is strangely defined by the "abnormal" behavior of others. Because the self relies on notions of the other and lacks real experience, the self defines everything relying on feelings or emotion. One might say that this is the ultimately lopsided binary self, one that no longer defines what it is or isn't, but only what it isn't.

The Media Equation

In the book *The Media Equation* (1996), Byron Reeves and Clifford Nass use the extensive research that they and their students at Stanford have compiled to show that people treat computers and television like other people. In other words, the study of mass communication is interpersonal in nature. Findings regarding how we act toward one another are successfully applied to human media relationships.

The media equation harkens back to McLuhan's beliefs that we react to technology and not necessarily content. However, instead of us shaping the technologies, the theorists believe that we are drawn into the media, or in Baudrillardian terms, seduced. Reeves and Nass argue that "media are full participants in our social and natural world" (p. 251). The authors say that this is because our brains cannot evolve as fast as technology, therefore we act toward technology as we would another person. Or better yet, as in the real world, we are attracted to others who are like us and, therefore, we must see ourselves in our electronic technologies. This is a strong example of our current relationship to technology and the postmodern self.

The media equation brings back strong, direct effects. But here again direct effects, as in the other cognitive theories, is from an internal enemy, a self that constructs a mediated self. Again, we see this as an otherly, blameless, and autonomous self. Both of the above theories further entrench or codify the teleself as a world builder, eraser, and re-creator. The self in this way becomes very intimate with technologies.

As I finished these paragraphs, a godsend of support for this notion came from *Time* magazine's 2006 "Person of the Year" edition. The cover had a picture of a computer with a reflective material on the screen. The issue announced the person of the year as "you." The caption continued, "Yes, you. You control the information age. Welcome to your world." What better way to welcome in the era of the media equation or what *Time* called Web 2.0?

Most of the features were about young people who either made millions on websites on which individuals can post information or about the people doing the posting. All of the articles seemed to be a bit tongue in cheek, evidenced by choosing personalities that were strange, to say the least, and/or by couching the subjects of the story as expert wasters of time and money.

The most salient article, by Josh Tyrangiel, was on the last page. He used parallels between the new Web 2.0 era to Andy Warhol's life. He says that the new age has erased Warhol's prediction of everyone having fifteen minutes of fame. Self-promotion and fame are the key to the new age. He writes, "as cameras shrank and screens multiplied, the barriers to fame would be . . . eradicated." He continues saying that everyone has become psychological Warhols who suffer from "acquired situational narcissism. When you were with him (Warhol), you'd feel as if he didn't have the slightest interest in knowing you. All he wanted to know was what you thought of him—or that you thought of him (attributed to Dr. Robert B. Millman)." Critic Harold Rosenberg said that Warhol was "the figure of the artist as nobody, though a nobody with a resounding signature." In his own words, Tyrangiel writes:

> There's something admirable and uniquely American in the act of self creation—but it helps if you actually create something. In a conceptual artist, cultivating emptiness falls within the acceptable bounds of schtick. (Even Warhol's originals were reproductions.)
>
> But Warhol also put his blankness behind a series of conspicuous velvet ropes, turning a democratic notion—we're all stars, or at least we all could be—into something toxic.

That which is toxic is the empathy one must gain in putting themselves on the web, because most of us have nothing to say. The new prophesy then is that people will no longer be famous for fifteen minutes. "On the web, everyone is famous to fifteen people."

Releasing the Free Agent

McLuhan wrote of the explosion of technology and its relationship to an imploding understanding of place, i.e., the global village. As the geographic locale expands, what we think of as local becomes smaller and more personal. Baudrillard's ideas on consumption and the nature of the postmodern individual mirror the logic of the implosion and explosion. Consumption in this case mirrors the very real explosion of information. It is true that we consume more products because of information, but it is more important to realize that we consume information. Consuming mere information creates an even greater illusion of technological explosion. However, when we consume information alone, we are consuming less and less meaning. Or at least Baudrillard believes that the explosion of information neutralizes information (1983a). As information explodes, meaning implodes.

Information devours its own contents; it devours communication and the social, and for two reasons: 1) Instead of causing communication, it exhausts itself in the act of staging the communication; instead of producing meaning, it exhausts itself in the staging of meaning (1983a, pp. 97-98) . . . 2) Behind the exacerbated staging of communication, the mass mass media, with its pressure of information, carries out an irresistible destruction of the social (p. 100).

The staging of communication is the act. This is the branded effect. The package overwhelms any need of meaning-making. This is important. This is more than just saying that packaging has become more important than the product in an age of the image and image-making. It also goes further than saying that the information of the packaging deletes any meaning at all, the point is that meaning-making has been corrupted.

This creation of a corrupted mass media logic or language leaves us at a loss to describe the social. Baudrillard refers to it as the "catastrophe of meaning" (p. 103). But he warns that there is no resolution or revolution to save us from this particular catastrophe. Beyond meaning, there is fascination, which results from the neutralization and implosion of meaning. Everything is reduced to titillation, obscenity, and pornography.

We can only be left with ways to define our privatized self. The individual has the sense of explosion of the self—a world of greater explanation and variety. However, variety at a certain point, to put it bluntly, becomes schizophrenic, the sense that one thing is happening and actually the opposite is true; but there is no distinction between the two directions. Choice (exploding) is, concurrently, reduced to one attribute (imploding).

The new universe relies on connections, feedback, and interface; its processes are narcissistic and involve constant surface change. The scene and the mirror no longer exist; instead, there is screen and network; the era of consumption has given way to the era of connections and feedback. Media invades, public space disappears. Private space also disappears (implosion/explosion). The one is no longer a spectacle, the other no longer secret. There is no difference between exterior and interior (Sarup, p. 164).

More and more information and less meaning, refusal of meaning replaces action and choice. We are in an era of implosion, of the collapse of previous differences, distinctions with no hierarchies. There has been a transformation from stable referents to "floating signs" (p. 167). Hyperreality dissolves the old oppositions; it does not transcend or resolve them. More real than real has become the only existence.

Media practices have rearranged our senses of place and time. Television is "real world"; television is dissolved into life, and life is dissolved into television. The fiction is "realized" and the "real" becomes fictive. Simulation has replaced production (the medium is the message).

The personalization of objects leads to a kind of privatization of the individual. Individuals are "privatized" (p. 165). Objects respond to the individual's perceived needs. The individual, through his collection of things, then represents him or herself through the perceived unique amalgam of things. Baudrillard says:

> it is clear that in the act of personalized consumption the subject, in his very existence on being a subject, succeeds in manifesting himself only as an object of economic demand. His project, filtered and fragmented in advance, is dashed by the very process that is supposed to realize it. Since "specific differences" are produced on an industrial scale, any choice he can make is ossified from the outset; only the illusion of personal distinctiveness remains (p. 152).

"The possession of objects frees only possessors, and always refers us back to infinite freedom to possess more objects; the only progression . . . is up the ladder of objects . . . that leads to nowhere" (p. 154). Baudrillard continues:

> There is a kind of inevitability at work here. Once a whole society articulates itself around models and focuses on them; once production strives in every way possible towards the systematic breaking down of models into series, and series in their turn into marginal differences or combinative variant, until at last objects come to have status just as ephemeral as that of words or images; once the systematic stretching of series turns the whole edifice into a paradigm, but a paradigm whose ordering is irreversible, in that the ladder of status is fixed and the rules of the game of status are the same for everyone; once we fall under the sway of this managed convergence—all negation becomes possible. There are no more overt contradictions, no more structural changes, no more social dialectics . . . Everything is in movement . . . yet nothing really changes. This is a society whose embrace of technological progress enables it to make every conceivable revolution, just so long as those revolutions are confined within its bounds. For all its increased productivity, our society does not open the door to one single structural change (p. 155).

This is the making of a free agent of a new sort, a free agent with no choice. Free agents who are only free agents through their creations in an object world. Free agents with no society other than the one stimulated by, not structured by or conveyed through, the mass media.

Without the mass media there are no masses; without the masses there are no mass media. Baudrillard's formulation of the masses goes beyond "mass society theory," which denounces the masses as destroying authentic bourgeois culture, and the Frankfurt School, which sees the masses as stupefied by capitalist "culture industry." Masses do not make sense of culture—they are simulated by it (Baudrillard, 1983). Culture is taken out of the hands of the masses.

Debord agreed. The means are the same as the ends. Information is just information. In the twelfth thesis he writes that everything that appears is good: whatever is good will appear. In mass media studies (more specifically, from a functionalist perspective) this is the major way to describe something called "status conferral of the media." A parsimonious term, "status conferral" speaks to the postmodern phenomenon of "if something is important it will be the focus of mass attention, if it is the focus of mass attention it must be important." This attitude demands a passive acceptance, yet active participation. The spectacle has only to develop for itself. It has captive demand (e.g., thesis sixteen).

More directly, concerning the notion of the self, Debord believed that the spectacle has created a shift from being to having. Individuals define themselves not as being but as having. They define themselves, not just as materialists who collect objects, but by assuming social character. This is not to be confused with the notion that individuals are social characters. This has always been true. Here, we are saying that individuals assume social character. Individual realities exist. To appear as an individual is more important. This mirrors the market of signs, hyperreality, and theories of symbolic interaction or communicative action. In my mind, this marks the emergence of the branded character—the individual brand (self) not associated with the product (identity).

Debord paints a picture of the new individual that I will build upon. The individual constructs a self who, as we already know, is released from responsibility by the spectacle itself. He gets to philosophize outside of philosophy. Reality itself is philosophized, hyperrealized, or situationalized. The self-made reality—if the person is smart—is one of self-praise and self-adulation, not goal setting. Reality is depicted as whatever can most easily be delivered to the market.

In such a system, the old Marxist commodity is queer and trivial. The new mass media consumer doesn't fall victim to commodification. This notion might be liberating, but it is not. We fall for meaningless images. But then again, it works for what we've become. The arbitrariness of images and signs further releases us from being right, wrong, good, bad, true, false, etc. We live in a world in which ads do not have to show the product. This is evidence not only that we buy the signs, but more so that we do not attach meaning to our philosophized world.

Alas, our individuality, always in the spotlight, is that and only that: in the spotlight. The spotlight (now we have come to the meaning of the spectacle) functionalizes the human being. The social limits of the spotlight and playing to the spotlight are the individual. The social framework and its communicative action are the self. There is no freedom beyond this activity. We are proletariatized regardless of class, a function of the spectacle.

One last important observation. In the book *In The Shadow of the Silent Majorities*, (1983a) Baudrillard concludes that we are:

> an insoluble "double bind" like children face to face with an adult universe. They are summoned to behave like autonomous subjects, responsible, free, and conscious, and as submissive objects, inert, obedient, and conforming. The child resists on all levels, and to a contradictory demand he also responds with a double strategy. To demand to be an object, he opposes all the practices of disobedience, revolt, emancipation; in short, a total claim to subjecthood. To the demand to be a subject, he opposes just as stubbornly and efficaciously with an object's resistance, that is to say, in exactly the opposite manner: infantilism, hyper conformity, a total dependence, passivity, idiocy (p. 107).

Appendix

Poststructuralism and Critical Theory

From Kurt Vonnegut's *Slaughterhouse Five* on the end of the world:

> Billy Pilgrim: Someone accidentally pulled the switch.
> Miss Montana: Why did you let him?
> Pilgrim: Because that's how the moment was structured.

The goal of this appendix is to explain poststructural theory, which has been used to address the changing nature of the self. The problem is that poststructuralism is not a set body of theories. As a matter of fact, it isn't even a set body, let alone a theory or theories. Poststructuralism is a reaction to structuralism. At the same time, poststructuralism is anything that uses structural metaphors to describe contemporary culture. Poststructuralism, in other words could not have existed without either structuralism and cultural changes, which are antithetical or not described under modernism and are, therefore, postmodern. Poststructural theory is, therefore, very much a normative theory, arising out of the seemingly normal (or abnormal). It is really not the refinement or rejection of structural theory.

Therefore, this appendix begins with a description of structural linguistics as described in the field of semiotics. The two major branches, semiotics and semiology, are outlined. Poststructuralism is then put forth as a reaction to structuralism. The description is then fostered by the necessary categorical observation of the postmodern, the broad term used to describe contradictions to modernism. The appendix ends with a proposal to strengthen and enrich poststructural theory, both theoretically and methodologically, by considering the contributions of critical theory.

The type of structuralism spoken about here is a linguistic-based theory. Whether from the fields of economics, history, sociology, or psychology, structural theories posit underlying determinants (usually economic, social, or cultural) of social or psychological phenomena. Therefore, in this case "structural" implies that the structure of a language holds important meanings in itself, in most cases about larger structures, such as culture or society. "Poststructural" can mean many things, but for this work it has to do with the detachment of symbols from the things and ideas that they signify. Poststructuralism is not so much the denial or rejection of structuralism as it is the use of structuralism to look at breaks from past constructions of reality and eras, primarily from the modern to the postmodern.

Structural linguistics theories basically fall into two types or approaches: semiotics and semiology. The two types developed independently of one another and approach the topic of the sign from different points of view. However, many attributes from each theory are compatible. Both find their beginnings in the ancient study of symptomology, and both are attempts at some general understanding of the communication process. The semiology of Ferdinand Saussure privileged the act of communication to makes cultural analyses. The semiotics of Charles Peirce was concerned with vocabularies and the passing on of knowledge, thus in another way articulating particular cultures. In some ways the two are complementary as macro and micro analyses of linguistic structures.

Semiotics

Semiotics is concerned with how directly signifiers refer to the signified. Peirce, a late nineteenth-century logician, believed there are three categories of signs. The "iconic" sign directly resembles that for which it stands (a photo of a person). The "index" is associated with something it stands for (smoke for fire). The "symbol" is an arbitrary reference (words in general). Each category's utility is defined by its flexibility. Icons are the least flexible of signs. There is a much greater likelihood of one to one correspondence. Symbols are much more flexible than the other two types of signs.

The assumption that we can identify signs and that to which they correspond is the most important in semiotics. The idea of the flexibility or arbitrariness of signs is secondary to the ontological assumption that signs are direct empirical links to meaning. With this we can also assume that ideas result from an association with signs and that ideas can be assessed through the use of corresponding signs.

So, depending on the flexibility of the sign or its arbitrariness, Peirce was primarily concerned with meaning that arises when an idea or concept can be raised in the mind of the interpreter. In other words, correspondence is confirmed in how well the symbol used matches the expectations of the person receiving a sign. The "receiver" in semiotics is an interpretant who holds ideas. Representatmen are the signs.

Representamen stood for objects to the idea or interpretants. The model looks like Figure A.1:

Semiotics of Peirce

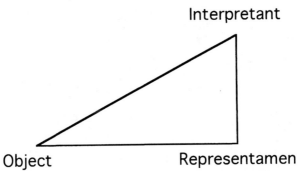

Figure A.1.

This model is interpreted at two levels of representation. First, it represents the stability of signs. Is a sign connected to an object? In this representation, the interpretant represents the ideas that confirm the relationship's truth or falsity. The model can also be used as a simple communication model in which we view the relationship of ideas to objects in the interpretant. How well does the interpretant, a person or receiver, understand the representation? We can see the model from the point of view of the sign as utilitarian or from the point of view of the human interpretant as receiver.

With this in mind we can go one step further. We can assume that the person is the accumulation of experiences or his contact with signs and their associations. Experience is the key here. Experience assumes a historical position. With this assumption, we can build a communication model. Peirce called communication the process of semiosis. It may be represented by Figure A.2:

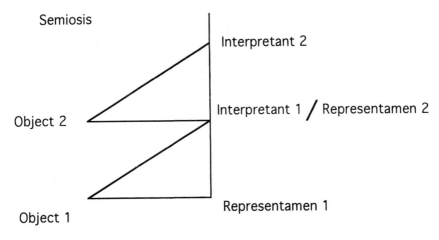

Figure A.2.

The model continues on upward as a representation of two processes. First, imagine a receiver of a sign trying to make sense of it. He matches it with other ideas and it does not match, so he tries again. The idea is a bit more complex, but there are remnants of the previous ideas to either help or hinder the understanding at the next attempt. This is represented in the combination "interpretant 1/representamen 2" level. Meaning is a process of potential infinite regression. In this internal conversation of matching and eliminating associations, the interpretant as receiver comes to some kind of understanding, which can include misunderstanding.

At another level, the level of communication, the same model used to represent the process of conversation, can be used. When we converse there is a general assumption that the purpose is to reduce uncertainty. Uncertainty is reduced in the emotional and psychological domains. In order to do this, however, there is a general process in which we come to understand one's talk, references, and patterns. These are things that must be understood or "agreed" upon before other types of uncertainty can be reduced. "Meaning is always deferred, always becoming through contrast between the sign and its interpretant" (Gottdeiner, 1995, p. 11).

The process of semiosis then lends itself to communicative behaviors if we limit those behaviors to the act of matching up one idea to another. A communicator is good when he or she understands what his or her audience understands. The operative word "what" still alludes to concrete, realist imagination. Second, and more useful to us, is how the model represents the ongoing process of understanding in social situations or how a sign may change through history.

Semiology

Saussure, a linguist, was interested in the meaning given to signs. Saussure defined a sign as composed of two parts: a signifier, or the carrier of the sign (e.g., the spoken word), and the signified, the meaning called forth by the signifier. But instead of assuming a concrete relationship between the two, Saussure believed that both changed constantly with the use of the other. Both the signifier and the signified shape one another and are always present together. This "dual unity" of the sign in semiotics insubstantiates any notion of a concrete relationship between components: sign and what it represents, though logically bound, remain elusive to any rigorous analytic strategy. In this way semiology defines an idealistic philosophy versus Peirce's realism. In other words, our world is a product of our thoughts and signs and does not "live" separate from us. This is represented in this way:

Signifier <——> Signified

Meanings are of two types: denotative and connotative. Denotation refers to the stability of the dual unity of the sign; that is, if the sign worked well as a signifier of the signified. Instead of being interested in the stability between signifier and how well it represents a real object or reality in general, Saussure wanted to know how well the signified is related to the signifier and vice versa.

Semiologists go beyond simple understanding of signs as bound to just one moment in time or one discourse act. Saussure used the terms "parole" and "langue" to explain. Parole is the speech act or the individual act of discourse. Langue is the cultural component outside the individual that shapes how we perform in these speech acts. It is the study of these relationships that Saussure used in his analysis of language to learn more about cultural phenomena. In the chain of relationship one might boil it down to: Words are to sentences are to discourse as signs are to socialization is to culture. Signs are more of a reference to discourse and culture than to a thing represented.

Connotative analyses examine the systematic relationship among parts as dictated by structure (langue). On one hand, there is the relationship between and among signs that implies meaning. Semiologists believe that structure is doubly articulated—that signs always have at least two relationships, such as in the signifier/signified relationship, as can be visualized in the model. At the connotative level, signs, in this case words, can be analyzed using two dimensions. In the paradigmatic axis, words have relationships with other words. For example, one could choose to use the word "cat" in a sentence. Another choice could have been "feline." The choice of "cat" as the best word for the occasion is part of the semantic realm of the paradigmatic axis. There is also another relationship and that is the connotation of "cat," the word chosen, and the words not chosen. This is called the synchronic relationship of language on the paradigmatic axis. What is used is related to what could be used and says this relationship says something about the meaning.

Words, as signs, also connote meaning from one to another in a given sentence. This axis of meaning is called the syntagmatic. Meaning is connoted through the relationship of words, one to another in a sentence, commonly known as syntax. Each word gives additional meaning to the sentence and other words. There are two subdimensions of the syntagmatic axis. Diachronic relationships to the syntagmatic axis suggest order, time, action, sequence itself, and so on. The position of the words themselves determine a set meaning. They follow the accepted logic or pattern of the culture. This is called the metonomic dimension of syntax.

Together the syntagmatic and paradigmatic axes comprise the structure of language. Their presence constitutes a system of signification which arises due to the combinatory rules of association and juxtaposition. The socially accepted rules make up the code. From the semiological perspective, "all cultural phenomena are systems of signification because they are structured according to the relations and contrasts of both the syntagmatic and paradigmatic axes" (Gottdiener, 1995, p. 7).

Roland Barthes strengthened Saussure's linguistic theories, expanding them into cultural theories. He particularly used semiology to analyze the nature of signs in both ideology and myth. For example, a Rolex represents at the connotative level, or second level of the sign, upper-class membership, but at the same time supports the separation of classes. In this relationship, what is said about the relationship is at two levels. The direct or first level is class member-ship. The second level refers to the separation of class. This concept of nega-tion—what appears also describes what does not appear—was furthered by Al-girdas Greimas (1976).

Barthes reasoned from connotation to talk about the cultural level, rather than the structural (langue) level. This is important. If we allow connotation to refer to culture, culture itself, as a living thing, becomes richer. What we con-note changes within the situation. At the same time, it allows for polysemy. Polysemic signs have multiple meanings. More specifically, however, the idea of polysemy is that a sign conveys all its possible meanings when uttered.

This dynamic works even further back in the "meaning chain," making de-notative relationships more dynamic. Signs are both structured and structuring. Here, he builds on the dual unity aspect but adds that the structuring that goes on is a perfect representation of the interaction between language and culture. The relationship that signs have to that which they signify is culturally embedded. A word not only names an object but in some ways delimits the object. A package of soap signifies its contents, while at the same time it "packages" our concep-tion of the product (imagine a soap powder called sludge).

Let's compare semiotics and semiology. Semiotics is normative and obser-vational. Semiology is a more generalized theory of signs. Semiotics is a product of the age of empiricism. Semiology is a product of critical, anti-industrial movements; therefore, it extends analysis to natural languages, literature, myth, legends, politics, etc. Semiotics values ontologies of the real, while semiology values ideal creations of the mind and setting.

In both semiotics and semiology, signs are arbitrary. However, each uses the term arbitrary differently. Semiotics is concerned with how well things are represented (icons and indexes). A sign's arbitrariness refers to how well it rep-resents. Arbitrariness in semiology is about why signs represent things or ideas. Why a sign is used to refer to something tells us about its possible historical, political, and cultural implications. Social construction in signs matters in that "If men define situations as real, they are real in their consequences" (Rochberg-Halton, 1986, p. 44). Again, signs are both structured and structuring.

Knowing the meaning of a sign means understanding its cultural power; this is a big leap made by semiology over semiotics. But as its own name suggests, semiology attempts to explain underlying causes that may possibly give us a greater clue to our own humanness.

In my attempt to build a profile of the teleself, I borrow liberally from both semiology and semiotics. At this point, I maintain what semiology attempts to say about the relationships of signs to culture and ideology. I believe that semi-ology creates many more useful metaphors for proceeding with descriptions of the postmodern world. A linguistic-based theory will fit the linguistic turn bet-ter. As we will see, it is also necessary to talk about signs that exist on their own, not apart or anchored to an idea or concrete object. In short, I appreciate the ide-alist philosophical grounding of the theory. Semiology is a theory about the mode of communication (Gottdiener, 1994). It is about the formation of social relationships, which are our realities.

On the other hand, I will also borrow from the semiotic model. If we want to talk about the transformation of the self, we must use a model that includes the self or a position for the individual. As a mode of information model, one that depicts the "flow" of information, the model includes a receptor and is much more parsimonious than semiology's model, which means it is more streamlined and more manageable (however it may or may not be more isomorphic, i.e., closeness of fit to real life).

What's more, Peirce suggested that things could be signs and that signs could be things. Derrida points this out (1976) in his criticism of semiology. Derrida appreciates the semiological idea (or, more appropriately, poststructural semiology) that signs can stand alone as representative, but says that this does not explain the social-historical phenomena that creates such signs—the mark of postmodernism. Peirce's idea of semiosis is much better, in Derrida's mind, for describing socio-historical processes.

First, we can imagine how this is used in interaction. When one tries to understand, he or she tries to match the new sign with similar ideas that he may already hold. The process of semiosis then lends itself to communicative behaviors if we limit those behaviors to the act of matching up one idea to another. A good communicator is such because he or she understands what his or her audience understands. The problem here is that the operative word "what" still alludes to a very concrete, realist imagination. Second, and more useful to us, is how the model represents the ongoing process of understanding in social situations or how a sign may change over time.

In the end, I like the idealist and communicative attributes of semiology. I also appreciate the stronger historical links of poststructuralism and postmodernism to semiology. However, I believe that the model of semiotics presents, no matter how artificial, a clearer representation of the individual's place in the process of interpretation and in the socio-historical process of semiosis. The model that I will use later in this work depends on showing the position of the self across contextual changes, i.e., romantic, modern, and postmodern and pre-industrial, industrial and postcapitalist.

Poststructural Semiotics and Postmodernism

Barthes can be given the credit for leading semiology to its limits. During a trip to Japan, Barthes was overwhelmed by the emphasis on product packaging. Barthes noticed that packages of products had little to do with the product contained in them. Barthes realized that words do not have to exist for objects; they can, but most of all, they exist because language exists. This would soon become a major theme of poststructuralists who argue that signs have become disconnected from that which they signify, or at least have gained their own importance.

Poststructural semiotics took Barthes's lead and went further, arguing that signs are no longer bound by a single culture and can explain more than their referents. Not only are signs polysemic, signs have broken away from the signified and may only represent itself or represent an illusion of the existence of something.

A poststructural sign is anything that "can be used to significantly stand for something else" or "to lie" (Eco, 1976). This definition in its broadest sense could be used to identify almost anything and everything as a sign. In a more narrow sense, however, it helps us identify signs that are used to tell greater lies about the reality. Therefore, signs that are taken for granted as merely mirroring the things they signify, especially when those things are so closely representative of the major product (read: popular culture) of the dominant ideology (read: capitalism), are the most important signs for discussion. Signs are ideological in themselves.

Characteristics of the Postmodern

So what are the dominant observations that lead us to believe that we are in a shift from the modern to a postmodern culture? Jameson (1983, 1984) outlines six characteristics of postmodernism. They are: 1) a break with established and dominant forms; 2) the blurring of low and high culture distinctions; 3) depthlessness; 4) fragmentation or schizophrenia; 5) emotional subjectivity; and 6) a deep relationship with new technologies.

The first characteristic is that postmodernism reacts against dominant established art forms. In order for any movement to distinguish itself as "new" this point is obvious. However, the way in which postmodernism establishes itself as new is not to create anything new. The point is to repeat and fuse the old and tired. Postmodernism reacts not in a way to create new forms but to blur the distinctions of past forms and of high, low, folk, popular, and any other class distinctions of the forms. Representations need not rely on one period style or on one level of abstraction. Romantic poetry could be mixed and matched with the modernist—a mix of both periods and levels of discourse. Postmodern architecture fuses international style with Georgian features—a fusing of periods and levels of formality. In this way, postmodernism is an extension or critique of modernism.

Depthlessness has to do with the interpretability of a representation. One cannot look at the representation, whether it is an advertisement, painting, music video, etc., and "situate its features into a life-context" (Jameson, 1995, p. 89). The work itself rejects being associated strongly with any reality. Postmoderns use the word "simulacrum" to refer to this form. A simulacrum is a representation for something that never existed. In our era of late capatalism we have come to so strongly assume that representations represent things that we no longer question the validity of the reference, the ideology, metaphysical, or whether the thing referenced even exists. A simulacrum only represents itself.

Not only does the postmodern ignore historical reference, any type of historical progression or coherent storytelling is rejected. "Pastiche" dominates. Often associated with the "MTV style," pastiche describes the combination of unrelated representations, and that which they might represent to one another or to a thing or idea. The point is no longer to tell a story, but to combine and repeat unrelated representations that illustrate either only an esthetically pleasing quality (they just look good together) or a schizophrenic, fragmented quality that further confuses the link between the signifier and the signified. The object becomes questionable as to its purpose or meaning. But what is more is that style obliterates any sense of time or direction and metaphor turns on itself. In other words, a line of postmodern poetry (called language poetry) might not contain words that logically follow one another. The effect is confusion about its adequacy as a poem and its sense of "natural" order defined by the conventions of the sentence.

The result of these phenomena is emotional subjectivity. Fragmentation in the representation implies a fragmentation of the audience. It permits the audience to believe that all interpretation is personal, unmindful, anti-intellectual, and, dominantly, emotional. It follows in a world without history, purpose, or meaning, that only subjectivity and emotional value exist. When art forms are evaluated primarily on their feel-good qualities, emotions are all that matter.

Lastly, mass media technologies did not make postmodernism possible. Trends in deindustrialization planted the seed. However, mass media technologies hastened the advance of postmodernism by saturating the everyday world with so many signs that the value of signs became as important or more important than that which they represented. Of course, this leads to competition between signs, not products, and their increased repetition. To this point, mass media remain just a tool. However, postmodernity has fixed its gaze on the repetitious nature of machines. All notions of machines of production are gone. The next machine will be one that repeats the same thing faster and better, not a machine that creates a new product or refines an old one.

Critical Theory

In this section, I want to discuss the critical theory movement and its purpose. The reason for this section is the need to attach formal historical theory to the normative theory of poststructuralism.

Like poststucturalism, critical theory grew out of a sensitivity to the times and a lack of explanation of contemporary events by other theories. Critical theory is more of a movement than one theory.

Critical theory promotes the project of emancipation by furthering the theoretical effort of the critique of domination begun by the Enlightenment and continued by Marx. As a type of neo-Marxism, critical theory is a reaction to the shortcomings of Marxism and an attempt to understand three modern phenomena: 1) the establishment of bureaucratic socialism in Eastern Europe; 2) the rise of fascism in Central Europe; and 3) the birth of the "culture industry" in Western Europe and the United States (Poster, pp. 1-2). These massive phenomena reshuffled the deck for cultural theorists. No longer could it be said that the working class is the standard-bearer of freedom. The third point is of most importance to the present research.

Critical theory, most closely associated with the Frankfurt School, was dominated by Adorno, Horkheimer, Herbert Marcuse, and, eventually, Jürgen

Habermas. In their early years, Adorno, Horkheimer, and Marcuse continued the concerns of Marx. They set out to liberate, as Marx had. However, two major forces of Marxism were transformed. First, critical theory focused on the dominance of mass culture as a social control, rather than on production. Critical theorists argued that people were no longer dominated by any specific means of production or by any conscious manipulations of a more general mode of production. People were viewed as manipulated, depoliticized, and reconciled to capitalistic values by all aspects of popular culture. Second, the Frankfurt School spoke about the product of popular culture as mass culture: the "masses." No longer were workers addressed as the oppressed majority. The general public was made unitary through their focus on vulgar mass cultures.

The Frankfurt School continued toward the goals of the Enlightenment: to remind the masses to be conscious of the discourse used to control them. In retrospect, however, in speaking to and about the masses, an unavoidable condescending tone emerged. The masses became the "other" of the Frankfurt discourse. In their work, the "Frankfurt School staged contemporary life as a parody of crude capitalist greed and stupid working-class gullibility" (Poster, p. 2). And when this "other" had no concrete means of production (whatever it was that made them stupid), the Frankfurt School appeared elitist and pedantic.

Problems mounted. Because there was little thought given to what coordinated the manipulation and the industries involved, critical theory often sounded conspiratory. At other times, the argument was hollow in its broad, functionalist categorical claims.

Soon afterwards the Frankfurt School gave up on the masses. As a matter of fact, they seemed to have given up on not only class conflict and class itself, but on the notion of the individual. Adorno's "negative dialectic" emerged. In opposition to a sense of synthesis or revolution, the mode of "negative dialectic" postulated a non-identity of the subject. Critique turned away from emancipation and toward a last-ditch effort to save something in a world already doomed by the first Frankfurt movement.

Adorno and Horkheimer recognized that the discourse of popular culture is the key to modern domination. Knowing about what is popular with others gave the masses of the modern age a sense of belonging to something greater (but useless and frivolous in the eyes of the Frankfurt School). Popular culture discourse not only dominated the modern: the modern age dominated popular culture. Scientific themes were constructed and dumbed-up for the masses. Politics became a participatory sport rather than a pluralistic activity.

Critical Theory and Poststructuralism

This brings me to the initial grounding of my approach. I am particularly interested in the study of discourse in relation to stages of capitalism. I am interested in Horkheimer's analysis of the discourse he called scientism and Adorno's study of popular discourse. This goes back to something I have reiterated in this book. I believe that the postmodern is an extension of the modern, a stage. The postmodern is grounded in the production of the popular culture, especially the self-referential self.

Critical theory and poststuctural theory both grew out of theories of the modern age. Critical theory grew out of Marxism, a type of structural theory. Poststuctural theory grew out of linguistic structuralism. Both theories grew out of their predecessors not so much because the latter had stalled but because the times had outgrown them.

The theories also outgrew the Enlightenment's and modernism's focus on the ontological. Critical theory and poststructuralism rely on the epistemological domain. The assumption is that ways of knowing contribute to definitions of human nature. Critical theorists attempt to uncover the sense of knowledge or, better, "knowing," given to the masses. Of course, critical theorists still operate in the ontological to build assumptions of the construction of the masses. But because they are now masses and not workers any longer, forms of knowledge and not the nature of the individual, are much more important to investigate. Adorno's and Horkheimer's focus on an investigation of popular discourse caused a shift to greater reliance on the epistimological domain for their own discourse.

Poststructuralists emphasize epistemology more than most contemporary theorists. Poststructuralists attempt to clarify the connections between the metaphysical and the real. Poststructuralists worry that we have placed too much faith in theorists' abilities to make determinations free of the political. In the real world, the poststructuralist imagines him or herself as an arbiter of sense-making. This is similar to critical theory's demands to assess the basis of knowledge. The postmodern theories are directed toward theorists themselves, instead of being applied to the masses of the critical theorists, those who interpret the links between the metaphysical and the real, as suppressors of the masses. Therefore, the ontological is left unimportant.

But one might say that the poststructuralists go one step further in annihilating ontology. The self or the ontological question "what is it to be human?" has been boldly answered. That answer is a straightforward structuralist answer that posits linguistic structures as the root of humanness and the determinants of thought. Poststructuralism, like its poor sister, postmodernism, is more of a philosophy of theory that spills over as comment on reality. Poststructuralists are particularly concerned with the foundations and limits of theory itself (Poster, p. 15).

Poststructuralists, like the critical theorists, address the centrality of discourse. Baudrillard offers to decode the new age of "hyperreality" in which self-referential mass media languages constitute simulacra of communications. Derrida proposes an interminable deconstruction of Western philosophical tradition. Jean-François Lyotard celebrates multiple, competing discourses, an acceptance of the justice of the differend, of the impossibility of consensus. Foucault proposes the self-constitution of the critical through a practice of opposition to the dominant discourses of the present.

Fredric Jameson, a Marxist, has embraced the point of view of poststructuralism. There is no longer a Marxian gap or rift between classes or knowledge and the real. The concept of ideology no longer works. The radically new space of postmodernism, which undermines all efforts of self-location, of referential self-coordination, requires entirely new categories of thought, an "aesthetic of cognitive mapping" in order to achieve "a breakthrough to some as yet unimaginable new mode of representing . . . in which we may again begin to grasp our positioning as individual and collective subjects and regain a capacity to act and struggle, which is at present neutralized by spatial as well as our social confusion."

Jameson calls "cognitive mapping" the link between discourse and society. The mind may be a mirror of the real or vice versa, but the discourse distorts one or the other or both. The most probable explanation is that discourse is entirely a construct of the real but is more real because we use it to represent all other realms including itself to each other daily.

Critical theory has much to offer poststructural theory and vice versa. Critical theory can lend a historical aspect lacking in poststructural theory and its observational database, postmodernism, and poststructural theory can revive the negative endeavor that it has become. For example, poststructuralists reevaluate the nature of the self and conclude that the new subject is conceptualized through language. They also question the use of language as representative of anything of the real. If indeed this is right, what better theory than critical theory to unmask the dimensions of power represented in language? At another level, how can the language of the theorist be "real"? Critical theory in its focus on the construction of the real world by scholarly ideas (especially science and politics) can be used as a checks and balances system to analyze academic discourse or at least reveal its arbitrary nature in relation to its public dependency and believability.

Foucault is important because of his integration of poststructural theory and critical theory. Although he rejected both labels, Foucault held attitudes that fit in both camps. First, he might be considered a critical theorist because of his emphasis on history and its discourse mode of discovery. He was a poststructuralist because of his interests in the relationship between history and the development of the public notion of the self.

Foucault's philosophy of the self moved from the dispersal of the subject in discourse to the issue of the constitution of self. A centered self could only once again become a possibility, only the self was understood in socio-historical, not ontological, terms. Early works argued from an archaeological critique of the self as rationalist by strategy of reversal: madness versus reason. This position mirrored a semi-traditionalist view of structuralism and its emphasis on the binary opposition to uncover layers of knowledge regarding historical eras. From this grew a genealogical critique of the self as centered consciousness by a strategy of displacement; the locus of intelligibility shifted from subject to structure. Consciousness was defined by social structures. This position fit traditional structuralist views and early critical theory. Lastly, Foucault came to a position he called ethics. A hermeneutics of the self using a strategy of historicism; Foucault's emphasis was on self-constitution in discursive practices (Poster, 1989).

This progression of ideas reminds us of the transitions in the development of critical theory and the structural to poststructural shift.

Foucault eventually believed that we create ourselves as works of art. Foucault studied the discursive practices by which the self establishes the "truth" of itself in the relation it has with itself. This was similar to Friedrich Nietzsche's belief that the self is not given or fixed, but a creation of each individual.

Now the Kantian ideal self that comes into being as an unconnected being is nothing new. However, Foucault sees a different kind of self-constitution. The major difference is that instead of arguing a real versus ideal or structural versus phenomenological construction of the self, Foucault argued that the idea of the self-constitution is a historical phenomenon that is very new to human experience altogether. He argued that individuals did not exist as we know them today until the Enlightenment. It was during the Enlightenment that beings recognized that personal identity cannot be separated from the fate of humanity, and this fate is understood as historically constituted. In this sense maturity designated the degree of authenticity of the individual's connectedness with the world. Maturity to Foucault meant understanding that we cannot escape our heritage from the Enlightenment. We must try to proceed with the analysis of ourselves as beings who are historically determined, to a certain extent, by the Enlightenment. At the same time we discover we are inseparable from our society and history, we discover ourselves.

Since that time, the self in history may be reconstructed as such: Liberalism treats the subject as an autonomous, rational, often presocial individual, wary of its rights in relation to other individuals. Marxism treats the subject as a collective agent in contest with other agents. In both cases the subject is grounded in history. By the late twentieth century both positions have become unconvincing. Liberalism's subject as citizen and entrepreneur and Marxism's subject as revolutionary proletariat no longer work as characters in the play of human time.

In writing the "future of the now," "criticism is no longer going to be practiced as the search for formal structures with universal value, but rather as a historical investigation into the events that have led us to constitute ourselves and to recognize ourselves as subjects of what we are doing." The subject becomes an active agent, a point of intelligibility, a self that constitutes itself in relation to history. Jean-Paul Sartre spoke of self-creation as the process of consciousness in which values or meaning are inserted into the world. The ego or self is the sum of its projects, of meanings hoisted upon nothingness.

Habermas's view on the constitution of the individual is similar. The critical scholar's subject differs from Marxist views by privileging communications over labor. If the conditions of "the ideal speech situation" are fulfilled, the subject emerges as a rational agent within the intersubjective realm of speech acts. Habermas's subject is also not quite the Enlightenment's subject by a Hegalian turn. Habermas historicizes the individual in terms of moral development. This mirrors Foucault's "ethics" period.

The Critical Turn, or What Do We Do Now?

The idea of social psychology as history can be fostered by a concrete approach. The purpose if to also, now that we have discussed the changing nature of the self, to give life to Gergen's call to return to the central mission of social psychology and that is the study of the self.

We have interesting postmodern phenomena to observe. However, theories of control and prediction are needed. I believe that we can find this in certain strains of critical theory. Critical theory enables us to do two things. The first is that critical theory is a theory of history that fits the thesis that all histories are interpreted in a cultural context of both the past and present. Second, it follows then that critical theory is discourse centered in method.

Go back to my reference to evolution. I said that we are not talking about evolution in simple "survival of the fittest" terms. I said that evolution was the refinement of an existing system. Well, I believe I was right but I would not want to argue that point based only on my simple definition of human evolution. My definition is too focused on biological and psychological mechanisms. To talk about communication as a biological and psychological developing tool is, for me, too narrow and one-sided. However, we cannot ignore them.

Identity is determined in many ways and must be understood through various methods. As Jacques Lacan believed, phenomenology stresses a free self; structuralist emphasis is the language determinant. In conservative or traditional theoretical circles this might appear to be a contradiction. However, in the postmodern, the stability of theory is in question. Therefore, theories are used for different levels of analysis and converge in explanations.

I mentioned culture, but only as a historical mechanism for remembering communicative action (Habermas). Culture is not just a representative past, it is also present and future. The rest of my definition includes the socio-historical refinement that constrains and acts as memory to our psychological and biological development.

Critical theory gives us a way to couch developments in communication in terms of a social history, more specifically, the history of now. Foucault attempts to "delegitimize the present from separating it from the past . . . demonstrating the foreignness of the past, relativizing and undercuts the legitimacy of the present."

> His Nietzchschean tactic of critique through the presentation of difference. . .
> begins with the present and goes backward in time until a difference is located.
> The alien discourses/practices are explored in such a way that their negativity
> in relation to the present explodes the "rationality" of phenomena that are taken
> for granted. When the technology of power of the past is elaborated in detail,
> present day assumptions which posit the past as "irrational" are undermined
> (Sarup, 1993, 56).

Foucault's critical theory rejects notions of historical epochs as replacements for the preceding historical epoch (survival of the fittest). This brand of critical theory does not speak to epochs or dialectical changes. The critical approach that I use here examines history as building on its past and refining what it has discovered. All "new" eras contain that which preceded them (Baudrillard, 1993; Attali, 1989).

However, through refinements of ideas and technologies, there is some alienation of past and present ideas, technologies, and social groups. So, I believe that evolution creates new, but only at the subsumation of the old, not its replacement or expense. At the same time, certain unused mechanisms are lost. For example, television is the embodiment of the oral, radio, and print. It has, however, technically lost some of its references to those other mass media as it has been reified into its own. It has created a homogeneous society by alienating, not differences among people, but difference itself.

The Twenty-First Century meets Continental Philosophy

The twentieth century gives prominence to language and enacts drastic changes in the structure of language. Electronically-mediated language experiences substantially alter the ways in which the individual structures the self. The individual constitutes him or herself as a consumer; in this way, the mode of information strengthens the hegemonic forces.

But the individual must also play with the very process of self-constitution; in this respect, the mode of information undermines the cultural basis of dominant structures. All these experiences enact asynchronous discursive practices that heighten the self-referentiality of language and undermine the earlier stability of the subject, the sense of having a continuous identity rooted in time, in space, and in relation with others and things. "The anonymity of high-tech 'conversations' elicits a play of multiple self-identifications" (Poster, p. 69). The subject becomes his or her own object of knowledge through electronically mediated changes.

Paradoxically, like no other theory or all other theory of the contemporary (we will not know), both critical theory and poststructural theory are creations, reactions, and victims of their times. Both are adequate comments on phenomenon. Both are highly reflexive and suspicious of their own ability to contaminate their observations. Both are their own best supporters and enemies.

For the current work, poststructural theory explains observations of postmodern phenomena that are the result of a saturated linguistic or communicative world. Critical theory gives a sense of history and meaning of self-reflexivity to the postmodern observations. I see good theory as being descriptive, explanatory, and predictive. Postmodern theory describes the phenomena around us very well. It gives a mechanism of explanation on which critical theory fell short. Critical theory gives a sense of evolution and history to the postmodern. It helps show where the poststructural, as the theory, and postmodern, as the era, fit. In the end the critical approach may help us predict the results (although, in the postmodern they may be negative dialectical or non-results) of the postmodern.

References

Althusser, L. (1969). *For Marx*. London: New Left Books.

Anderson, J. A. (1996). *Communication theory: Epistemological foundations*. New York: Guilford Press.

Attali, J. (1989). *Noise: The political economy of music*. Minneapolis: University of Minnesota Press.

Barthes, R. (1967). *Element of Semiology*. New York: Hill and Wang.

Baudrillard, J. (1983a). *In the shadow of the silent majorities*. New York: Semiotext(e).

———. (1983b). *Simulations*. New York: Semiotext(e).

———. (1981). *For a critique of the political economy of the sign*. St. Louis: Telos Press.

Bellah, R. N., Madsen, R., Sullivan, W. M., Swindler, A, and Tipton, S. M. (1985). *Habits of the heart: Individualism and commitment in American life*. New York: Harper and Row.

Beniger, J. R. (1987). Toward an old new paradigm: the half-century flirtation with mass society. *Public Opinion Quarterly* 51, S46-S66.

Best, S. & Kellner, D. (1991). *Postmodern Theory*. New York: Guilford Press.

Bishop, R. C. (2006). The whole world is watching, but so what? A frame analysis of newspapercoverage of anti war protest. In Nikolaev, A. G. & E. A. Hakanen. *Leading to the 2003 Iraq war: The global media debate*. New York: Palgrave Macmillan.

Blumer, H. (1969). *Symbolic interactionism*. Englewood Cliffs, NJ: Prentice-Hall.

———. (1979). *Critiques of research in the social sciences: An appraisal of Thomas and Znanieck's "The Polish peasant in Europe and America."* New Brunswick, NJ: Transaction Books.

Bryant, J. & Thompson, S. (2002). *Fundamentals of media effects*. New York: McGraw-Hill Co.

Carey, J. W. (1967). Harold Adams Innis and Marshall McLuhan. *The Antioch Review*. 27(1), 5-39.

Carey, J. W. (1996). The Chicago school and Mass communication research. In Dennis, E. E. & E. Wartella (Eds.). *American communication research: The remembered history*. Mahwah, NJ: Erlbaum.

Csikzentmihalyi, M. & Rochberg-Halton, E. (1981). *The meaning of things: Domestic symbols and the self.* Chicago: University of Chicago Press.

Curran, J., Gurevitch, M., & Woollacott, J. (1982). The study of the media: Theoretical approaches. In Gurevitch, M., T. Bennett, J. Curran, & J. Woollacott (Eds.). *Culture, Society and the Media.* London: Methuen.

Czitrom, D. J. (1982). *Media and the American mind: From Morse to McLuhan.* Chapel Hill: The University of North Carolina Press.

Dale, E. (1935). *The content of motion pictures.* New York: Macmillan.

D'Angelo, P. (2002). New framing as a multiparadigmatic research: A response to Entman. *Journal of Communication* 52, 870-888.

Davidson, W. P. (1983). The third-person effect in communication. *Public Opinion Quarterly.* 47:1-15.

Deborg, G. (1994). *The society of the spectacle.* New York: Zone Books.

DeFleur, M. L. & Ball-Rokeach, S. (1989). *Theories of mass communication.* New York: Longman.

Dennis, E. E. & E. Wartella (eds.) (1996). *American communication research: The remembered history.* Mahwah, NJ: Erlbaum.

Denzin, N. K. (1992). *Symbolic interactionism and cultural studies.* London: Blackwell.

deSola Pool, I. (1980). *Technologies of Freedom.* Cambridge, MA: MIT Press.

Durham, M. G. & D. M. Kellner (Eds.). (2001). *Media and cultural studies: Keyworks.* Oxford: Blackwell.

Eco, U. (1976). *A theory of semiotics.* Bloomington: Indiana University Press.

Ellul, J. (1964). *The Technological Society.* New York: Vintage.

Ennis, P. H. (1992). *The seventh stream: The emergence of rocknroll in American popular music.* Hanover, NH: Wesleyan/New England University Press.

Finnegan, R. (1975). *Literacy and Orality: Studies in the Technology of Communication.* Oxford: Basil Blackwell.

Fish, S. (1987). *Is there a text in this class? The authority of interpretive communities.* Cambridge, MA: Harvard University Press.

Fiske, J. (1992). British Cultural Studies and Television. In Allen, R. C. (Ed.), *Channels of Discourse, Reassembled.* London: Routledge.

Foreman, H. J. (1933). *Our movie-made children.* New York: Macmillan.

Foucualt, M. (1970). *The order of things: An archaeology of the human sciences.* New York: Vintage.

———. (1972). *The archeology of knowledge and the discourse on language.* New York: Vintage.

———. (1982). The subject and power. In H. L. Dreyfus and P. Rabinow (Eds.), *Michel Foucault: Beyond structuralism and hermaneutics.* Chicago: University of Chicago Press.

Frith, S. (ed.), (1988). *Facing the music.* New York: Pantheon.

Gadamer, H. (1975). *Truth and method.* New York: Seabury.

Gamson, W. & Modigliani, A. (1987). The changing culture of affirmative action. In *Research in Political Sociology* (Vol. 3), Braungart, R. D. (Ed). Greenwich, CT: JAL.

Gandy, O. H. (2001). Epilogue. In Reese, S., O. H. Gandy, & A. Grant. *Framing public life.* Mahwah, NJ: Lawrence Erlbaum and Assoc.

Gerbner, G., Gross, L., Morgan, M., & Signorielli, N. (1986). Living with television: The dynamics of the cultivation process. In Bryant, J. & D. Zillmann (Eds.), *Perspectives on media effects: Advances in theory and research.* Hillsdale, NJ: Lawrence Erlbaum.

Gergen, K. J. (1991). *The Saturated Self: Dilemmas of Identity in Contemporary Life*. New York: Basic Books.

———. (1973). Social psychology as history. *Journal of Personality and Social Psychology* 26:2, 309-320.

———. (1996). Social psychology as social construction: The emerging vision. In McGarty, C. & A. Haslam (Eds.), *The message of social psychology: perspectives on mind in society*. Oxford: Blackwell.

Gottdiener, M. (1995). *Postmodern Semiotics: Material culture and the forms of postmodern life*. Oxford: Blackwell.

———. (1994). Semiotics and postmodernism. In Dickens, D. R. & A. Fontana (Eds.), *Postmodernism and Social Inquiry*. London: Guilford Press.

Greimas, A. J. (1976). *Semiotics et sciences soliciales*. Paris: Seuil.

Graber, D. (1984). *Processing the news: How people tame the information tide*. New York: Longman.

Grossberg, L. (1992). *We got to get out of this place: Popular conservativism and postmodern culture*. London: Routledge.

Gurevitch, M., T. Bennett, J. Curran, & J. Woollacott (Eds). (1982). *Culture, Society and the Media*. London: Methuen.

Harland, R. (1988). *Superstructuralism: The philosophy of structuralism and poststructuralism*. London: Routledge.

Hacking, I. (1981). How should we do the history of statistics? *Ideology and Consciousness* 8, 15-16.

Hakanen, E. A. (1995). Emotional use of music by African American adolescents. *Howard Journal of Communication* 5(3). 214-222.

Heath, R. L. & Bryant, J. (2000). *Human communication theory and research: concepts, contexts, and challenges*. Mahwah, NJ: Erlbaum.

Hawkes, T. (1977). *Structuralism and semiotics*. Los Angeles: UCLA.

Horton, D. & Wohl, R. R. (1956) Mass communication as para-social interaction. *Psychiatry* 19, 215-29.

Jameson, F. (1994). *Postmodernism, or, the cultural logic of late capitalism*. Durham, NC: Duke University Press.

———. (1972). *The prison-house of language: A critical account of structuralism and Russian formalism*. Princeton, NJ: Princeton University Press.

Katz, E. (1980). On conceptualizing media effects. In T. McCormack (Ed.), *Studies in communication* (Vol. 1, 119-144) Greenwich, CT: Jai Press.

Katz, E. & Lazarsfeld, P. F. (1955). *Personal influence: The part played by people in the flow of mass communication*. Glencoe, IL: The Free Press of Glencoe.

Katz, E., Gurevitch, M., & Haas, H. (1973). On the use of the mass media for important things. *American Sociological Review* 38, 164-181.

Kuhn, T. (1970). *The structure of scientific revolution*. Chicago: University of Chicago Press.

Lasswell, H. D. (1948). The structure and function of communication in society. In L. Bryson (Ed), *The communication of ideas* (pp. 37-51) New York: Harper.

Lefevure, A. (1958). *Critique of everyday life*.

Levy-Strauss, C. (1966). *The savage mind*. London: Weidenfield and Nicolson.

Luke, C. (1990). *Constructing the child viewer: A history of the American discourse on television and children*, 1950-1980. New York: Praeger.

Lazarsfeld, P. F., Berelson, B., and Gaudet, H. (1948). *The people's choice*. New York: Columbia University.

Lasorsa, D. L. (1991). Political outspokenness: Factors working against the spiral of silence. *Journalism Quarterly* 68, 130-140.

Lowery, S. A. and DeFleur, M. L. (1988). *Milestones in mass communication research.* New York: Longman.

Lule, J. (2001). *Daily news, eternal stories.* New York: Guilford.

McCombs, M. & Shaw, D. (1972). The agenda setting function of mass media. *Public Opinion Quarterly*, 36, 176-85.

McLeod, D. M., Eveland, W. P. & Nathanson. (1995). Support for censorship of violent and misogynic rap lyrics: An analysis of the third-person effect. *Communication Research* 24(2), 153-74.

McLeod, J. M. & Becker, L. B. (1974). Testing the validity of gratifications measures through political effects analysis. In J. G. Blumer & E. Katz (Eds.), *The uses of mass communications: Current perspectives on gratifications research* (pp. 135-65). Beverly Hills, CA: Sage.

McLuhan, H. M. (1964). *Understanding media: The extensions of man.* New York: McGraw-Hill.

McQuail, D., Blumer, J. G., & Brown, J. R. (1972). The television audience: A revised perspective. In D. McQuail (Ed.), *Sociology of mass communicationst* (pp. 135-65). Middlesex, England: Penguin.

McQuail, D. & Windahl, S. (1981). *Communication models for the study of mass communication.* London: Longman.

Mendelson, H. (1963). Socio-psychological perspectives on the mass media and public anxiety. *Journalism Quarterly* 40, 511-16.

Noelle-Neumann, E. (1973). Return of the concept of powerful mass media effects. In H. Eguchio and K. Sata (eds.), *Studies in Broadcasting*, 67-82. Tokyo: Nippon Hoso kyokai.

————. (1980). Mass media and social change in developed societies. In G. C. Wilhoit and H. de Bock (eds.), *Mass Communication Yearbook.* Beverly Hills: Sage. 657-78.

————. (1993). *The spiral of silence: Public opinion—our social skin.* University of Chicago Press: Chicago.

Ong, W. (1982). *Orality and technology: The technologizing of the word.* London: Methuen.

Pacey, A. (1983). *The Culture of Technology.* Oxford: Blackwell.

Palmgree, P. & Rayburn, J. D., II (1982). Gratifications sought and media exposure: An expectancy value model. *Communication Research* 9, 561-80.

Pearlin, L. I. (1959). Social and personal stress and escape television viewing. *Public Opinion Quarterly* 23, 255-59.

Peters, C. C. (1933). *Motion pictures and standards of morality.* New York: Macmillan.

Peterson, R. C. and Thurstone, L. L. (1933). *Motion pictures and the social attitudes of children.* New York: Macmillan.

Poster, M. (ed.). (1988). *Jean Baudrillard: Selected writings.* Palo Alto, CA: Stanford.

————. (1989). *Critical theory and poststructuralism: In search of a context.* Ithaca, NY: Cornell.

————. (1990). *The mode of information.* Chicago: University of Chicago Press

Postman, N. (1993). *Technopoly: The surrender of culture to technology.* New York: Vintage.

————. (1983). *The Disappearance of Childhood.* London: W.H. Allen.

Reeves, B. & Nass, C. (1996). *The media equation: How people treat computers, television, and new media like real people.* New York: Cambridge University Press.

Richie, D. (1986). Shannon and Weaver: Unraveling the paradox of information. *Communication Research* 13(2), 278-98.

Riesman, D. (1953). *The lonely crowd.* New Haven, CT: Yale University Press.

Rochberg-Halton, E. (1986). *Meaning and modernity*. Chicago: University of Chicago Press.

Rogers, E. M. (1962). *Diffusion of Innovations*. New York: The Free Press.

———. (1994). *A history of Communication study: A biographical approach*. New York: The Free Press.

Rose, T. (1994). *Black noise: Rap music and Black culture in contemporary America*. Hanover, NH: Wesleyan/New England University Press.

Rosnow, R. L. (1981). *Paradigms in transition: The methodology of social inquiry*. New York: Oxford University Press.

Rothlisberger, F. J. & Dickson, W. J. (1939). *Management and the worker*. Cambridge, MA: Harvard University Press.

Rubin, A. M. (1984). Ritualized and instrumental television viewing. *Journal of Communication* 34(3), 67-77.

Rubin, A. M. & Perse, E. M. (1987). Audience activity and television new gratifications. *Communication Research* 14, 58-84.

Rubin, A. M. & Windahl, S. (1986). The uses and dependency model of mass communication. *Critical Studies in Mass Communication* 3, 184-99.

Salwen, M. B., Lin, C., & Matera, F. R. (1994). Willingness to discuss "official English": A test of three communities. *Journalism Quarterly* 71, 282-290.

Sanjek, D. (1991). *American popular music business in the 20th century*. New York: Oxford University Press.

Sarup, M. (1993). *An introductory guide to post-structuralism and post-modernism*. Athens: University of Georgia Press.

Severin, W. J. & Tankard, J. W. (2001). *Communication theories: Origins, methods, and uses in the mass media*. New York: Longman

Shannon, C. (1949). *The mathematical theory of communication*. Urbana: University of Illi-nois Press

Stephenson, W. (1967). *The play theory of mass communication*. Chicago: University of Chicago Press.

Tichi, C. (1991). *Electronic hearth: Creating an American television culture*. New York: Oxford.

Time. (Dec. 25, 2006).

Wagner, R. (1995). If you have the advertisement you don't need the product. In Battaglia, D. (Ed.), *Rhetorics of self-making*. 59-76.

Weaver, W. (1949). Recent contributions to the mathematical theory of communication. In C. Shannon and W. Weaver, *The mathematical theory of communication*. Urbana, IL: University of Illinois Press.

Weaver, D., Graber, D., McCombs, M., & Eyal, C. (1981). *Media agenda setting in a presidential election: Issues, images, and interest*. New York: Praeger.

Wiener, N. (1961). *Cybernetics, or control and communication in animal and machine*. Boston: MIT Press

Williams, R. (2001). Base and superstucture in Marxist cultural theory. In Durham, M. G. &, D. M. Kellner (Eds.), *Media and cultural studies: Keyworks*. Oxford: Blackwell.

———. (1954). *The human use of human beings*. Boston: Houghton and Mifflin.

Wright, C. R. (1960). Functional analysis and mass communication. *Public Opinion Quarterly* 24, 605-29.

Index

Adorno, Theodor, 1, 110, 111
agenda setting, 78–81
Althusser, Louis, 89
Anderson, James, 73, 74, 75, 76,
    81, 82
Attali, Jacques, 38, 39, 119
audience grid, 71–76, 94

Barthes, Roland, 105–6, 107
Baudrillard, Jean, 3,4, 5, 35–37, 38,
    40, 49, 61, 62–64, 71, 73, 76,
    80, 96, 98, 99, 115
Bellah, Robert, 11
Beniger, James, 78
Blumer, Herbert, 43, 45
Branded (television program),
    7–10, 11, 93

Carey, James, 23–24, 55
commodification, 2, 3, 6, 12, 13,
    35, 61, 62, 64, 77
Connors, Chuck, 8
Cooley, Charles, 44, 45
critical theory, 1, 5, 32, 52, 53, 59,
    78, 88, 110, 111, 114, 115
cultivation analysis (hypothesis,
    theory), 78, 82–84
cultural theory, 32, 35, 53, 59, 78,
    88
cybernetics, 28, 30, 31, 63, 68

Debord, Guy, 62–63, 98
Derrida, Jacques, 107
Diffusion of Innovations, 66
Durkheim, Emile, 72

Ellul, Jacques, 57, 58

Fiske, John, 90
Foucault, Michel, 2, 3, 4, 5, 15, 18,
    19, 20, 21, 72, 73, 113, 115
frame analysis, 84–85
Frankfurt School, 6, 40, 83, 110

Gerbner, George, 78, 82, 83
Gergen, Kenneth, 2, 15–18, 73, 80
Gramsci, Antonio, 89–90

Habermas, Jurgen, 110, 113, 114
Hall, Stuart, 89–91
Hocking, Ian, 72
Horkheimer, Max, 1, 110, 111
Hovland, Carl, 51
hypodermic effects. *See* magic
    bullet effects

information theory, 28–31
Innis, Harold, 55

Jameson, Fredric, 13, 73, 94, 108,
    112

Katz, Elihu, 65, 66, 68
Klein, Naomi, 1
Kuhn, Thomas, 3, 15, 17, 18, 22,
    23, 25

Lacan, Jaque, 114
Lasswell, Harold, 28, 50
Lazersfeld, Paul, 65, 66
learning theory, 51

Lefebvre, Henri, 61, 62
Levi-Strauss, Claude, 72
limited effect model, 24, 32, 51–52

magic bullet effects, 24, 32, 41–43,
    51, 52
Marx, Karl, 20, 32, 52, 53, 61, 89,
    90, 99, 110, 111, 113
McCombs, Maxwell, 78–80
McLuhan, H. Marshall, 3, 4, 37,
    55, 56, 57, 58, 59, 96
Mead, George Herbert, 44, 45
media equation, 95–96
media systems dependency theory,
    86–88
moderate effects, 24, 32
modernism, 13, 20, 36, 40

Noelle-Neumanne, Elizabeth, 78,
    81, 82

Payne Fund Studies, 40, 41–42, 45
Peirce, Charles, 102, 103, 107
Poster, Mark, 3, 4, 110, 112, 115
Postman, Neil, 3, 37, 58, 72
postmodernism, 3, 4, 5, 6, 12, 13,
    35, 38, 94, 95, 108–9, 115
poststructuralism, 4, 5, 6, 63, 75,
    101, 108, 111–12, 115

Rogers, Everett, 66
Rosnow, Ralph, 15, 16, 18

Saussure, Ferdinand, 102, 104, 105
semiology, 104–7
semiotics, 102–4, 107–8
Shannon, Claude, 5, 28, 30
Shaw, Donald, 78
Simmel, Georg, 43–44
simulacrum, 12, 36, 92, 108
Situationists, 62
social grid, 12, 16, 21, 22, 72, 73
spiral of silence, 81–82
surgeon general's report on media
    violence, 5
symbolic interactionism, 32, 35,
    43–46, 52

technological determinism, 55, 56
teleself, 5, 12, 13, 35, 71
The People's Choice, 66–67
third person effects, 94–95
Tichi, Cecilia, 25–26, 27
two-step flow, 52, 65–67

uses and gratifications, 27, 32, 35,
    68–70, 85

Weaver, Warren, 5, 28–29, 30
Wiener, Norbert, 5, 30, 31
Why We Fight Studies, 51–52
Williams, Raymond, 88